DATE DUE

GAYLORD		PRINTED IN U.S.A.

TRAINING THE POOR

TRAINING THE POOR

A Benefit-Cost Analysis of Manpower Programs in the U.S. Antipoverty Program

by

D. O. SEWELL

INDUSTRIAL RELATIONS CENTRE
QUEEN'S UNIVERSITY
at Kingston, Ontario

1971

TRAINING THE POOR: A Benefit-Cost Analysis of Manpower
   Programs in the U.S. Antipoverty Program

Copyright © 1971 by.David O. Sewell

Library of Congress Catalog Card Number: 72-115766

Research Series: No. 12

Printed and bound in Canada by: Hanson & Edgar, Ltd., Kingston, Ont.

FOREWORD

Cost-benefit analyses have increasingly been used in the decade of the 1960s to evaluate investments in human capital and operating programs in the manpower field. Professor Sewell's study examines an important area in this field — training the poor. Using cost-benefit analysis and extensive case studies, he assesses manpower programs in the U.S. antipoverty program. In view of the many current programs in this field, and the related large financial resources involved, Professor Sewell's study is particularly timely. It should contribute greatly to better understanding of this important field.

The author is Assistant Professor of Economics and Faculty Associate in the Industrial Relations Centre at Queen's University. His undergraduate work was done at the University of New Zealand, and his doctorate at Duke University.

The Director wishes to express his appreciation to Professor Sewell for preparing this excellent study for publication, and to Mrs. C. Williams and Centre staff for their valuable editorial work.

W. DONALD WOOD, Director,
Industrial Relations Centre,
Queen's University at Kingston, Ont.

November, 1970.

PREFACE

I have accumulated a number of obligations in the course of writing this study. My interest in the theory of investment in human capital was originally stimulated by Professor Joseph Spengler, and interest in the antipoverty applications of the theory developed when I was working at the North Carolina Fund in 1966-67.

Carol Van Alstyne was instrumental in encouraging me to undertake the analysis, and in obtaining an initial grant from the North Carolina Fund to enable me to assess the effects of Manpower Improvement through Community Effort (MITCE). The major proportion of the financial support for the study came from a grant to the North Carolina Fund from the United States Department of Labor,[1] and funds were also provided in the form of a Research Fellowship from the Industrial Relations Centre of Queen's University.

Bruce Jones and the staff of MITCE were unfailingly helpful in providing the background information and data necessary for the study. Dick Groner and Betti Goldwasser of the United States Department of Labor also provided moral and statistical support throughout the study, and its text benefited from a number of their suggestions. Charles Fairchild supplied valuable assistance in the organization of the survey of MITCE clients, and also performed the initial processing of the survey data. Lloyd Wilson subsequently programmed these data for further statistical analysis. I would also like to thank Mrs. Ellen McKay and Mrs. Ann Lacey for their pain-

---

1. Consequently, I am required to make the following formal acknowledgement:

The material in this project was prepared under a Grant from the Office of Manpower Policy, Evaluation, and Research, U.S. Department of Labor, under the authority of Title I of the Manpower Development and Training Act of 1962. Researchers undertaking such projects under Government sponsorship are encouraged to express freely their professional judgement. Therefore, points of view or opinions stated in this document do not necessarily represent the official position or policy of the Department of Labor. Reproduction by the United States Government in whole or in part is permitted for any purpose.

staking typing of the manuscript, and Mrs. Carol Williams and Mrs. Francesca Davenport for their efficient editing of the text.

I also owe a considerable debt to Harry Campbell, Neil Swan and Dan Usher for their comments on parts of the manuscript. Perhaps my greatest obligation in this respect is to my former teacher, Professor Frank Hanna, who provided encouragement and constructive criticism throughout the long antenatal period of the study.

I am well aware that acknowledgements for assistance can be a double-edged weapon. I would therefore like to make it abundantly clear that none of the parties I have mentioned should be held responsible for any remaining faults in the analysis.

DAVID O. SEWELL

November, 1970.

CONTENTS

LIST OF TABLES

CHAPTER I

INTRODUCTION

REASONS FOR INVESTMENTS IN HUMAN CAPITAL IN CURRENT UNITED STATES ANTIPOVERTY PROGRAMS

The marked emphasis on expenditures for vocational training and education in current United States antipoverty programs may be ascribed to a conjuncture of circumstances. In the last decade, research into these and other "investments in human capital" has had an impact on most of the traditional fields of economics, and has had the by-product of stimulating interest in the problem of poverty. Indeed, in his presidential address to the American Economic Association in 1960, which has been described as "the birth of the economics of education",[1] Theodore W. Schultz specifically drew the attention of the profession to the uses of the concept of human capital in the understanding of poverty.[2] Developing this theme in a subsequent examination of poverty in the United States, Schultz concluded that:

> ... it would appear that there have been strong incentives to invest in man, and such investments will explain most of the observed decline of poverty. The poverty that remains is to a large extent the result of such investment opportunities being thwarted.[3]

Nor is it difficult to find reasons why investment in the human capital of the poor may have been thwarted. The funds necessary for investments in human capital may not be as readily available as those for investments in physical capital, because of differences in the comparative liquidity of the two types of investment. Individuals who wish to borrow funds for physical capital formation can offer the assets to be acquired as collateral for the loan, and these assets can consequently be liquidated by the lender in the event of default on the loan. On the other hand, potential lenders for the act of human capital

---

1. M. Blaug, *The Economics of Education,* 2 vols. (Harmondsworth, England: Penguin Books, 1968), 1:11.

2. Theodore W. Schultz, "Investment in Human Capital", *American Economic Review* 51 (March, 1961) : 14-15.

3. Theodore W. Schultz, "Investing in Poor People: An Economist's View", *American Economic Review* 55 (May, 1965): 520.

formation can obtain no such collateral, because the prospective investment will be embodied in the borrower, who cannot, of course, be sold in the event that he defaults on the loan. These institutional constraints in the labor market[4] may in practice mean that investments in human capital need to be financed largely from the resources of the investor and his family, and it follows that persons from lower income backgrounds will be at a substantial disadvantage in making such investments.

It has long been argued that public intervention designed to weaken the effects of these institutional constraints in the labor market by promoting equality of opportunity to invest in human capital could improve the allocation of resources in the economy, and thereby increase national income.[5] Public support for some forms of investment in human capital may also be justified on the grounds that such investments lead to "external" benefits for society as a whole, as well as those private benefits which are captured by the individual.[6] Such arguments provide the rationale for the present extensive public expenditures on some forms of investments in human capital, particularly education. Nevertheless, there are good reasons for thinking that these public expenditures have not eliminated "underinvestment" in the human capital of the poor. For instance, it is the children from low-income backgrounds who are less likely to complete an elementary or secondary school education, and the financial returns from completing these lower levels of education are usually estimated to be well in excess of the average returns from comparable private investments.[7] It would therefore appear that there are substantial and sound

---

4.   While it is more usual to refer to these constraints as capital market imperfections, the writer prefers the terminology used in the text, for reasons outlined by Stigler:

The limitations placed upon borrowers by law are hardly to be labelled imperfections-in-the-capital-market. With any reasonable use of language, this legal limitation on laborers' bargaining rights should be called an "imperfection-of-the-labor-market".

George J. Stigler, "Imperfections in the Capital Market", *Journal of Political Economy* 75 (June, 1967): 288.

5.   According to Alfred Marshall,

There is no extravagance more prejudicial to the growth of national wealth than that wasteful negligence which allows genius that happens to be born of lowly parentage to expend itself in lowly work. No change would conduce so much to a rapid increase of material wealth as an improvement in our schools, and especially those of the middle grades, provided it be combined with an extensive system of scholarships, which will enable the clever son of a working man to rise gradually from school to school till he has the best theoretical and practical education which the age can give.

Principles of Economics, 8th ed. (London: Macmillan, 1966), p. 176.

6.   Thus, it is thought that one of the social benefits of education is the creation of a more informed electorate. Similarly, training programs for unemployed youth have been promoted on the grounds that they may reduce the social costs of juvenile delinquency.

7.   For instance, Hanoch's estimates of the financial rates of return from education – often regarded as the best yet available – show that the rate of return to white males from completing elementary school is over 100 per cent, and the rate of return to white males who complete a high school education is 33 per cent in the North and 44 per cent in

reasons for the increased public support for investments in human capital undertaken in current antipoverty programs.

The emphasis on expenditures on investments in human capital in current antipoverty programs may also represent a concession to a more austere ethic. As Marglin has noted:

> ... the community may not find it wholly satisfactory to achieve a given redistribution of income by simply transferring cash from one individual to another ... the size of the economic pie and its division may not be the only factors of concern to the community – the method of slicing the pie may also be relevant.[8]

In actual fact, there appears to be widespread public aversion to the use of transfer payments as a means of reducing poverty, and a linked belief that the poor should be made better off by working. These attitudes – possibly derived from the Protestant Ethic – have been reflected in executive goals from the "War on Poverty" of the Johnson Administration[9] through the proposed "Workfare" or Family Assistance Plan of the Nixon Administration.[10] Where the objective given to executive agencies is " ... to change people from 'poor' to

---

the South. See Giora Hanoch, "An Economic Analysis of Earnings and Schooling", *Journal of Human Resources* 2 (Summer, 1967): 322. Hanoch's estimates of the rates of return from education are unadjusted for differentials in ability between persons with different levels of education, and would be reduced if this factor were taken into account. On the other hand, upward adjustments in these rates of return from elementary and secondary education are also indicated if one accepts Weisbrod's argument that this schooling has an "option value", in that it gives the student access to the "excess returns" from further education. By taking account of this option value, for instance, Weisbrod raises Schultz's estimate of the rate of return on elementary education from 35 per cent to 54 per cent. See Burton A. Weisbrod, "Education and Investment in Human Capital", *Journal of Political Economy* 70 (Supplement, October, 1962): 109-13.

8.   Stephen A. Marglin, "Objectives of Water-Resource Development: A General Statement", in *Design of Water Resource Systems,* ed. Arthur Maass *et al.* (Cambridge, Mass.: Harvard University Press, 1962), p. 63.

9.   Thus, according to the *Annual Report of the Council of Economic Advisers* for 1964,

> About $11 billion a year would bring all poor families up to the $3,000 income level we have taken to be the minimum for a decent life. The majority of the Nation could simply tax themselves enough to provide the necessary income supplements to their less fortunate citizens. ... But this solution would leave untouched most of the roots of poverty. Americans want to *earn* the American standard of living by their own efforts and contributions. It will be far better, even if more difficult, to equip and to permit the poor of the nation to produce and to earn the additional $11 billion, and more.

U.S., President, *Economic Report of the President, 1964, together with the Annual Report of the Council of Economic Advisers* (Washington, D.C.: Government Printing Office, 1964): p. 77.

10.   The proposed Family Assistance Plan of the Nixon Administration is intended to combine a guaranteed minimum annual income through transfer payments with incentives for the poor to obtain work or vocational training. Thus:

> The Plan would supplement the incomes of the poor whose wages are too low to meet the needs of their families, and of those who have difficulty working, or probably ought not to be working, such as women with low incomes who head families with young children. ...

Introduction

'nonpoor' *through their own efforts"*,[11] it is understandable that a premium should be attached to measures such as education and vocational training programs which have the potential of increasing the earning ability of the poor.

Evaluations of the Effects of Antipoverty Programs

Two comprehensive assessments of the effectiveness of programs similar to those undertaken in the antipoverty program have recently been published.[12] Contrary to expectations, there is little in these surveys by Ribich and the Institute for Defense Analyses to justify optimism about the value of expenditures on general education in raising the incomes of the poor. However, both of these surveys do conclude that expenditures on vocational training appear to be an effective method of increasing the incomes of the poor.[13] Evidence which has become available since these surveys were published also tends to confirm the conclusion that vocational training is a more effective

---

... able-bodied men who are not employed, and mothers of families with no such man at home and no children under 6, must register at the State Employment Office for training or employment as a condition of receiving their benefit. ...

U.S., President, *Economic Report of the President, 1970, together with the Annual Report of the Council of Economic Advisers* (Washington, D.C.: Government Printing Office, 1970), p. 64.

11. See Robert A. Levine, "Evaluation of Economic Opportunity Programs: A Progress Report", *Proceedings of the Social Statistics Section, American Statistical Association,* 126th Annual Meeting, 1966 (Los Angeles, California, 1966), p. 342.

12. Thomas I. Ribich, *Education and Poverty* (Washington, D.C.: The Brookings Institution, 1968); The Institute for Defense Analyses, *Federal Poverty Programs: Assessment and Recommendations,* Report R-116 (Arlington, Va.: The Institute for Defense Analyses, 1966).

13. Thus Ribich concludes that:

Vocationally oriented training, at least in the form of recent manpower training programs, exhibits a higher rate of payoff than does general education. The rates are sufficiently in excess of those computed for improvements in general education that it is difficult to dismiss this result as an accident due entirely to the particular estimating techniques used. . . .
. . . with the exception of job retraining, the ratio of financial benefits to financial costs for educational improvements is found to be generally less than unity and, as suggested . . . [by Ribich's earlier analysis] . . . unweighted benefit-cost ratios would have to be something in excess of unity before education could be regarded as clearly superior to transfers or other forms of direct help.

Education and Poverty, pp. 97-98. The survey of the Institute for Defense Analyses devotes less attention than Ribich to the effect of expenditures on general education of the type undertaken in antipoverty programs, but does assert that:

. . . training programs, except for older workers, are quite promising for alleviating poverty . . . the private returns to retrained workers are apparently substantial [and] . . . training programs are a relatively inexpensive way to raise the incomes of lower-income families.

Federal Poverty Programs, pp. 65-66.

method of raising the incomes of population groups of interest to the antipoverty program than are expenditures on general education.[14]

PREVIOUS BENEFIT-COST ANALYSES OF
MDTA-TYPE TRAINING PROGRAMS

The generalizations concerning the effectiveness of vocational training in the surveys of antipoverty measures by Ribich and the Institute for Defense Analyses are in turn based on benefit-cost analyses of training programs administered under the Manpower Development and Training Act of 1962 (MDTA), the Area Redevelopment Act of 1961 (whose training provisions were transferred to MDTA in 1965), and earlier state equivalents of such federal legislation. The literature on the effects of these MDTA-type training programs has become extensive in recent years. Six benefit-cost analyses of particular MDTA-type training projects have now been published: three separate analyses for the same training projects conducted in West Virginia,[15] and other analyses for training projects conducted in Connecticut,[16] training projects conducted in Massachusetts,[17] and a national sample of MDTA training projects.[18]

14.   Thus a study of the experience of a sample of males who were rejected for military service because of failure to pass the Armed Forces Qualification Test suggests that:
. . . the estimated payoff to more schooling is low for our sample group of low achievers. . . .
. . . The returns to training are large enough, however, to suggest the wisdom of expanding training facilities rather than simply urging school attendance.
W. Lee Hansen, Burton A. Weisbrod, and William Scanlon, "Schooling and Earnings of Low Achievers", *American Economic Review* 60 (June, 1970): 416-17.

15.   Glen G. Cain and Ernst W. Stromsdorfer, "An Economic Evaluation of Government Retraining Programs in West Virginia", in *Retraining the Unemployed,* ed. Gerald G. Somers (Madison, Wis.: University of Wisconsin Press, 1968), pp. 299-335; Gerald G. Somers and Ernst W. Stromsdorfer, "Benefit-Cost Analysis of Manpower Retraining", *Proceedings of the Seventeenth Annual Meeting, Industrial Relations Research Association* (Madison, Wisconsin, 1964), pp. 172-85; Ernst W. Stromsdorfer, "Determinants of Economic Success in Retraining the Unemployed: The West Virginia Experience", *Journal of Human Resources* 3 (Spring, 1968): 139-58. Additional detail on the West Virginia training programs examined in the above analyses is also given in a study by Harold A. Gibbard and Gerald G. Somers, "Government Retraining of the Unemployed in West Virginia", in *Retraining the Unemployed,* pp. 17-124.

16.   Michael E. Borus has reported on his benefit-cost analysis of Connecticut training programs in three publications: *The Economic Effectiveness of Retraining the Unemployed,* Research Report to the Federal Reserve Bank of Boston, No. 35 (Boston: The Federal Reserve Bank of Boston, 1966); "A Benefit-Cost Analysis of the Economic Effectiveness of Retraining the Unemployed", *Yale Economic Essays* 4 (Fall, 1964): 371-429; and "The Effects of Retraining the Unemployed in Connecticut", in *Retraining the Unemployed,* pp. 125-48.

17.   David A. Page, "Retraining under the Manpower Development Act: A Cost-Benefit Analysis", *Public Policy* 13 (1964): 257-67.

18.   Planning Research Corporation, *Cost-Effectiveness Analysis of On-the-Job and Institutional Training Courses,* PRC D-1297 (Washington, D.C.: Planning Research Corporation, 1967).

Introduction

Evaluations of the benefits of other MDTA-type projects have been published by a number of scholars,[19] and analyses of the MDTA program as a whole, and similar training programs financed under other federal legislation, have also been undertaken by legislative agencies.[20]

It is entirely understandable that a great deal of effort has been expended in analyzing the effects of MDTA-type training projects, and that the authors of benefit-cost analyses of training projects conducted under federal and state legislation which preceded MDTA have taken pains to generalize about the expected effects of MDTA training on the basis of their findings. From the inception of the MDTA program in 1962 through fiscal 1968, over a million persons had been enrolled in MDTA training.[21] The MDTA program has played a key role in the efforts of various federal administrations to provide training for the poor, and similar training programs directed to a low-income clientele have been created by means of additional federal legislation.[22] Nevertheless, it may be wondered whether there is any need for yet another benefit-cost analysis of MDTA training projects, in view of the existing wealth of detailed evaluations of such projects. The stimulus for our own proposed analysis of such a project was the conviction that past analyses have limited relevance to current MDTA training directed to the poor, and that the conclusions that have been drawn from these past analyses are in any event subject to question.

The problem in drawing conclusions from past benefit-cost analyses of MDTA-type training projects is that these analyses use data from a period before substantial changes were made in the structure and objectives of the MDTA

---

19.   The findings from several of these analyses will subsequently be cited in the present study. See particularly Glen G. Cain and Gerald G. Somers, "Retraining the Disadvantaged Worker", in *Research in Vocational Education*, ed. Cathleen Quirk and Carol Sheehan (Madison, Wis.: Center for Studies in Vocational and Technical Education, University of Wisconsin, 1967), pp. 27-44; Earl D. Main, "A Nationwide Evaluation of MDTA Institutional Job Training", *Journal of Human Resources* 3 (Spring, 1968): 159-70; Richard J. Solie, "Employment Effects of Retraining the Unemployed", *Industrial and Labor Relations Review* 21 (January, 1968): 210-25 (also reprinted in *Retraining the Unemployed*, pp. 193-211).

20.   See for instance U.S., Congress, Senate, Committee on Labor and Public Welfare, Subcommittee on Employment, Manpower and Poverty, "Manpower Programs in the Antipoverty Effort", by Garth L. Mangum, in *Examination of the War on Poverty*, Staff and Consultants Reports, vol. II, 90th Cong., 1st sess., 1967, pp. 235 *et seq.*

21.   U.S., Department of Labor, *Manpower Report of the President for 1969* (Washington, D.C.: Government Printing Office, 1969), p. 80.

22.   Perhaps the best known antipoverty training programs which are similar in conception to MDTA are the Neighborhood Youth Corps and the Work Experience Program. The latter programs were created under the Economic Opportunity Act of 1964. This Act was also amended in 1965 and 1966 to spawn a variety of MDTA-type programs directed to particular groups among the poor. The Job Corps, also created under the Economic Opportunity Act of 1964, is different in conception from these MDTA-type training programs, in that its objective is to train youths away from their home environment. A comprehensive description of the various training programs for the poor authorized under federal legislation other than MDTA is given in the *Manpower Report of the President for 1969*, pp. 97-119.

program. A principal factor leading to passage of the Manpower Development and Training Act of 1962, and of prior federal and state legislation authorizing some of the training projects studied in past benefit-cost analyses, was concern about the high unemployment levels prevailing in the late 1950's and early 1960's.[23] The emphasis in the early training projects financed under MDTA was consequently put on " . . . the training and rapid job placement of the previously jobless".[24] This objective led MDTA officials to be highly selective in choosing trainees for projects conducted in the early years of MDTA. Entry to these training projects was usually conditional upon the applicant obtaining a high enough score on aptitude and intelligence tests, and passing other formal and informal selection criteria. Equally stringent selection criteria appear to have been employed in the training projects studied in past benefit-cost analyses which were authorized under earlier federal or state legislation similar in intent to MDTA. The attrition rate among applicants for training as a result of these selection processes could be quite severe; rejects comprised 64 per cent of all applicants for one course studied in a previous benefit-cost analysis.[25]

The significance of the selection procedures employed in these projects, of course, was that individuals who were less able or amenable to training were thereby culled out of the training process; to use a simile frequently encountered in discussion of these early MDTA-type programs, the trainees comprised the "cream" of the applicants for training. On these grounds alone, it could be argued that the benefit-cost analyses of these early MDTA-type programs are of limited interest to the antipoverty program. The trainees in the projects analyzed might have been expected to have risen out of a temporary situation of having low incomes without the aid of training subsidized by the government. The individuals who were excluded from training as a result of the selection criteria employed in these projects, on the other hand, comprised precisely those who might be expected to have low incomes in the long run.

The early MDTA program was also limited in other respects: for instance in its geographical coverage of the population, and in the type of training it

---

23. See for instance, *The Manpower Development and Training Act of 1962,* as amended, 42 U.S. Code 2571-2620, sec. 101.

24. *Manpower Report of the President for 1969,* p. 76.

25. See Borus, *Economic Effectiveness of Retraining the Unemployed,* p. 55. The mean ratio of rejections to total applications for the seven training courses studied by Borus was 39 per cent. As Borus remarks, "The aptitude requirements appear to have been very important in determining eligibility for the courses" *(ibid).* For the effects of the selection criteria in the various West Virginia training courses studied in previous benefit-cost analyses, see Gibbard and Somers, "Retraining in West Virginia", pp. 56-57. The presence of stringent selection criteria in the training programs studied in other benefit-cost analyses can also be inferred from the text of these analyses. See for instance Page, "Retraining under the Manpower Development Act", p. 267.

provided. Few services were extended to individuals living in rural areas.[26] In addition, little use was made of the on-the-job training provisions of MDTA; in the first three fiscal years of the program's operation, more than 90 per cent of the individuals enrolled in training were given classroom instruction in vocational schools (institutional training).[27] To a large extent, the benefit-cost analyses of early MDTA-type training projects reflect similar biases. Only one previous analysis deals with on-the-job training, and little attention is devoted in these analyses to the problems encountered in training persons living in rural areas. As we shall see, the latter problems can be radically different from the problems typically encountered in urban MDTA training projects.

The failure of the MDTA program to train the "hard-core unemployed" and those considered to be "disadvantaged" in the labor market led to successive amendments to the Manpower Development and Training Act in 1963, 1965 and 1966, designed to remedy these deficiencies. This formal redirection of the objectives of MDTA culminated in 1966, when it was announced that as a national goal, 65 per cent of all MDTA trainees were to be drawn from the "disadvantaged". Those considered to be disadvantaged in the labor market comprised youths, members of minority groups, persons with limited education, the rural poor, the long-term unemployed, and older workers. It was also announced in 1966 that on-the-job training was to receive greater emphasis in the MDTA program; in future, roughly 50 per cent of MDTA enrollees were to be trained on-the-job.[28] By the end of fiscal 1968, the objectives of both enrolling greater numbers of the disadvantaged and training more MDTA enrollees on-the-job appear to have been fulfilled.[29]

It is clear that the changes noted above in the structure and objectives of MDTA mean that the findings of previous benefit-cost analyses have to be severely qualified if they are to be used as a guide to the allocation of resources in the current MDTA program. Indeed, these changes in the structure and objectives of MDTA, and the creation of new MDTA-type programs for the purpose of training the disadvantaged population, have led some observers to conclude that, "at present, very little is known about the effectiveness of these programs in raising the earnings of the groups they serve", and consequently that

---

26.

... According to a spot-check survey of the MDTA Program by the Rural Community Development Service in 1964, only 3.4 per cent of its training projects were conducted in small towns under 10,000 population and in the rural areas they serve, and only 3.1 per cent of the total number of trainees who participated were in rural and small-town training projects.

C. Edwin Gilmour, "The Facts about Rural Poverty" (Address to the National Association for Community Development Conference on Rural Poverty, Washington, D.C., 1967), p. 4.

27.   See the *Manpower Report of the President for 1969*, p. 238.

28.   A concise account of the changes in the focus of the MDTA program noted in our text is given in the *Manpower Report of the President for 1969*, pp. 77-78 and 89-90.

29.   See the *Manpower Report of the President for 1969*, pp. 79 and 90.

the new antipoverty training programs also require completely new benefit-cost analyses.[30]

However, the writer would argue that the conclusions drawn from the benefit-cost analyses of early MDTA-type programs are, in any event, subject to question. Insofar as previous benefit-cost analyses examined the returns to society from MDTA-type training programs, they were primarily interested in the issue of whether these programs were efficient in an allocative sense; that is, whether the training of workers added more to output than the costs of goods and services forgone because training was undertaken. If the allocative benefits from training programs exceed their allocative costs, the policy implication from the use of this "efficiency" criterion is that training programs should continue to be undertaken by society. On the other hand, if the allocative costs of training programs exceed their allocative benefits, the corresponding policy implication is that no further public expenditures on these programs are warranted. All previous benefit-cost analyses of MDTA-type training programs concluded that these programs were allocatively efficient. Indeed, the benefit-cost ratios found in some of these studies are of a magnitude which suggest that, as a social investment, these training programs would only be rivalled by research breakthroughs such as the development of hybrid corn.[31] However, the conclusion that the MDTA-type training programs studied in former benefit-cost analyses were allocatively efficient will subsequently be challenged in the present study.

In their emphasis on efficiency criteria in assessing public expenditures, and their comparative disregard of the impact of these expenditures on the distribution of national income, past benefit-cost analyses of MDTA-type training programs have reflected a bias which is common in benefit-cost evaluations of public expenditures. It has long been argued on theoretical grounds that benefit-cost analyses of public programs must take into account their distributional consequences as well as their effects on the allocation of resources in the economy,[32] and we will attempt to put these precepts into

30. See Worth S. Bateman, "An Application of Cost-Benefit Analysis to the Work-Experience Program", *American Economic Review* 57 (May, 1967): 81. Other writers subscribing to this point of view include the coauthors of benefit-cost analyses of early MDTA-type training programs. See, for instance, Cain and Somers, "Retraining the Disadvantaged Worker", pp. 27-44.

31. For instance, Borus estimates that the social benefit-cost ratio of the training he studied could have been as high as 137:1. See *Economic Effectiveness of Retraining the Unemployed,* p. 84. While no other benefit-cost analysis of MDTA-type training programs arrived at such favorable results, other analysts also remark that the social returns from the projects they studied were nevertheless " ... extraordinarily high". See Cain and Stromsdorfer, "Retraining in West Virginia", p. 324. For the social returns from the invention of hybrid corn, see Zvi Griliches, "Research Costs and Social Returns: Hybrid Corn and Related Innovations", *Journal of Political Economy* 66 (October, 1958): 419-31.

32. See for instance Otto Eckstein, "A Survey of the Theory of Public Expenditure Criteria", in *Public Finances: Needs, Sources and Utilization,* ed. James M. Buchanan, National Bureau of Economic Research Special Conference Series No. 12 (Princeton, N.J.:

Introduction

practice in undertaking our own benefit-cost analysis of an MDTA training project. Of course, it might be argued that the distributional consequences of MDTA-type training programs are reasonably apparent, and consequently require little elaboration. The obvious implication of previous benefit-cost analyses is that these training programs made those who were poor better off. The examination of the findings of these previous analyses undertaken in the present study will suggest the need for caution in arriving at such judgements. Indeed, we will argue that the training projects studied in previous analyses may actually have been regressive in their impact on the distribution of incomes.

MANPOWER IMPROVEMENT THROUGH COMMUNITY EFFORT

Doubts about the relevance of past benefit-cost analyses of MDTA-type training programs, and the conclusions of these analyses, led the writer to undertake a benefit-cost analysis of an MDTA project which was considered to deal with a population of primary concern to the antipoverty program. The project studied, Manpower Improvement through Community Effort (MITCE), was an Experimental and Demonstration project financed under MDTA and sponsored by the North Carolina Fund.[33] While the MITCE project was actually in existence in the period 1964-67, data requirements restrict our analyses to training undertaken in the first of the project's contracts with the United States Department of Labor, in the period 1965-66.[34]

Princeton University Press, 1961), pp. 446-48; Arthur Maass, "Benefit-Cost Analysis: Its Relevance to Public Investment Decisions", *Quarterly Journal of Economics* 80 (May, 1966): 208-26; Stephen A. Marglin, "Objectives of Water-Resource Development: A General Statement", pp. 62-87; Burton A. Weisbrod, "Income Redistribution Effects and Benefit-Cost Analysis", in *Problems in Public Expenditure Analysis,* ed. Samuel B. Chase Jr. (Washington, D.C.: The Brookings Institution, 1968), pp. 177-209.

33. The North Carolina Fund was an antipoverty foundation incorporated in 1963 with an initial budget of $9.5 million. Under its articles of incorporation the Fund's objectives in its five-year life were

... to study the problems involved in improving the education, economic opportunities, living environment and general welfare of the people of North Carolina, of all ages and in different parts of the state; to make and recommend grants for research, pilot, experimental and other projects toward the solution of such problems; to make available professional staff services to private and public agencies, both state and local, seeking solutions to such problems; to encourage cooperative state and community action in devising such solutions; and to encourage wise use of public and philanthropic funds devoted to any of these purposes.

34. One of the primary requirements of a benefit-cost analysis of training programs is to obtain as long an income history as possible for workers after they complete their training. The necessary income data for MITCE clients were gathered in a 1967 survey, in effect restricting our analysis to training undertaken in the first MITCE contract. While this contract was for the period October, 1964 through June, 1966, it should be noted that no MITCE clients were trained before June, 1965. See Manpower Improvement through Community Effort, *Final Report under U.S. Department of Labor Contract No. 82-32-30* (Durham, N.C.: The North Carolina Fund, 1967), pp. 51 and 64. (This report will subsequently be referred to as the *MITCE Final Report.)*

It will be observed that the MITCE project was initiated before the MDTA program was formally redirected to focus on the training of disadvantaged members of the labor force. However, since the inception of MDTA, the Experimental and Demonstration projects financed under the Act have been principally directed towards the disadvantaged.[35] MITCE was one of the largest Experimental and Demonstration projects undertaken through 1967, and was also the first large-scale Experimental and Demonstration project designed to deal with the problems of the rural poor. In the latter respect the project's location in North Carolina was particularly appropriate: of all the fifty states, North Carolina ranked 45th in terms of per capita income and 46th in terms of the proportion of population living in urban areas at the time of the 1960 Census of Population.[36]

Characteristics of the Population in the MITCE
Target Areas and of the MITCE Clientele

The main objective of MITCE, as specified in the project's original contract with the U.S. Department of Labor, was to experiment with

> uses of the Manpower Development and Training Act programs for severely disadvantaged rural workers residing in areas of long economic decline, low levels of education and family income, high rates of out-migration and severe cultural problems which restrict the effectiveness of training and other manpower services.[37]

Table 1 leaves no doubt that the six eastern North Carolina counties in which the MITCE project was conducted met the quantifiable criteria specified in the contract. We should also note that 50 per cent of all families in these counties had incomes of less than $3000 in 1959. Thus, a large proportion of the inhabitants of these counties would have been considered within the scope of the antipoverty program using the definition of poverty first adopted by the Council of Economic Advisers.[38] However, the conditions of eligibility for training in MITCE were more stringent than the poverty qualification suggested by the Council of Economic Advisers. MITCE trainees were required to be heads of households, at least eighteen years of age, and prior to enrolment in training

---

35.

E & D projects were the first segment of MDTA operations to concentrate on the disadvantaged, to work at identifying their characteristics and needs, and to demonstrate the feasibility of training them. The findings have been of considerable help in implementing the redirection of regular MDTA training programs toward service to the disadvantaged.

Manpower Report of the President for 1969, p. 210.

36.   U.S., Department of Commerce, Bureau of the Census, *Statistical Abstract of the United States, 1967* (Washington, D.C.: Government Printing Office, 1967), pp. 17 and 327.

37.   *MITCE Final Report*, p. 3.

38.   See the *Economic Report of the President, 1964*, p. 58.

Introduction

Table 1: Characteristics of the Population
in the MITCE Target Area Counties

Counties	Net migration rate 1950-1960	Median grade level attained by adults 25 years and older in 1959	Per cent of families with less than $3000 in income in 1959
Craven	- 5.8	9.9	40.4
Edgecombe	- 9.0	7.8	51.1
Nash	- 7.3	8.0	48.6
Richmond	-14.3	8.4	40.0
Robeson	-16.2	7.9	60.1
Scotland	-14.0	7.6	51.3

Sources: U.S., Department of Commerce, Bureau of the Census, *United States Census of Population: 1960*, vol. I, *Characteristics of the Population*, pt. 35, *North Carolina* (Washington, D.C.: Government Printing Office, 1963), pp. 278-83; U.S., Department of Agriculture, Economic Research Service, *Net Migration of the Population, 1950-60, by Age, Sex, and Color*, vol. I, pt. 3 (Washington, D.C.: Government Printing Office, 1965), pp. 473-93.

they had to have been unemployed for more than six months, or to have been members of farm families with incomes of less than $1200.[39]

The characteristics of MITCE clients who were available for training and who were considered to meet the above qualifications can be described, since client description forms were completed for all such persons encountered in a canvass of the MITCE target areas undertaken when the project was initiated.[40] Data from these client description forms are used in Tables 2 and 3 to compare MITCE trainees, North Carolina and United States MDTA trainees, and United States MDTA trainees who were receiving public assistance when they entered training, with respect to their income needs and their degree of disadvantage in the labor market. Welfare recipients were included in the comparisons because they are usually considered to have greater income needs and to be more disadvantaged in the labor market than other MDTA trainees.[41] The characteristics used to illustrate the economic needs of trainees in Tables 2 and 3

39.   See the *MITCE Final Report*, p. 3.

40.   The "client description form" was the U.S. Department of Labor MDTA form No. MT-101. Client description forms were actually filled out for *all* those whom MITCE considered eligible under the terms of the contract. Some members of this population, however, were not available for training because of extreme age, grave physical disabilities, family responsibilities or because they had moved out of the area before MITCE followed them up. These groups were excluded from the population in coding the forms.

41.   See for instance Gerald G. Somers, "Evaluation of Work Experience and Training of Older Workers" (Report to the National Council on the Aging, University of Wisconsin, Industrial Relations Research Institute, 1967), p. 13.

Table 2: Per Cent Distribution of Characteristics of MDTA Trainees in 1965: The United States, North Carolina and MITCE

Characteristic	United States Inst.[1]	United States OJT[2]	North Carolina Inst.	North Carolina OJT	MITCE Inst. & OJT
Sex	100.0	100.0	100.0	100.0	100.0
Male	60.0	75.6	77.4	38.5	77.1
Female	40.0	24.4	22.6	61.5	22.9
Family status	100.0	100.0	100.0	100.0	100.0
Head of family	51.4	48.5	56.1	43.0	95.9
Other	48.6	51.5	43.9	57.0	4.1
Age	100.0	100.0	100.0	100.0	100.0
Under 21 yrs.	42.0	39.2	38.2	25.6	23.2
21 to 44 yrs.	48.0	50.9	52.4	56.9	63.5
45 yrs. & over	10.0	9.9	9.4	17.5	13.3
Education	100.0	100.0	100.0	100.0	100.0
Under 8 grades	7.1	4.2	16.2	8.9	28.9
8 grades	9.9	7.9	12.9	8.7	10.3
9 to 11 grades	33.9	26.2	26.2	30.5	35.4
12 grades & over	49.1	61.7	44.7	51.9	25.3
Yrs. of gainful employment	100.0	100.0	100.0	100.0	100.0
Under 3 yrs.	42.7	40.0	31.7	36.8	34.3
3 to 9 yrs.	34.9	37.0	42.7	35.5	35.0
10 yrs. or more	22.4	23.0	25.6	27.7	30.7
Labor force status[3]	100.0	100.0	100.0	100.0	100.0
Unemployed	86.2	63.2	84.1	31.2	39.4
Family farm worker	1.8	0.9	13.5	0.2	37.2
Entrant to labor force	3.6	2.3	0.1	3.4	7.1
Underemployed	8.4	33.6	2.4	65.1	16.4
Duration of Unemployment	100.0	100.0	100.0	100.0	100.0
Less than 5 wks.	32.8	40.6	43.1	40.1	4.4
5 to 14 wks.	23.3	26.1	16.2	14.4	24.5
15 to 26 wks.	13.2	12.4	7.6	9.0	35.7
27 to 52 wks.	11.0	8.9	6.0	9.9	25.2
Over 52 wks.	19.7	12.0	11.2	26.6	10.0
Color	100.0	100.0	100.0	100.0	100.0
White	66.3	79.3	49.1	71.2	11.8
Nonwhite	33.7	20.7	50.9	28.8	88.2
No. of dependents	100.0	100.0	100.0	100.0	100.0
0	47.0	45.8	43.7	38.2	15.7
1 - 3	38.0	41.2	33.8	53.4	44.0
4 or more	15.0	13.0	22.5	8.3	43.8

1. Institutional trainees.   2. On-the-job trainees.   3. Prior to enrolment in training.

Sources: U.S. data: U.S., Department of Labor, *1966 Report of the Secretary of Labor on Manpower Research and Training under the Manpower Development and Training Act of 1962* (Washington, D.C.: Government Printing Office, 1966), Tables 1, 12, A.9., A.11. North Carolina data: Employment Security Commission of North Carolina. MITCE data: U.S. Dept. of Labor Form MT-101.

Introduction

Table 3: Characteristics of All MDTA Trainees, Public Assistance MDTA Trainees and MITCE Trainees, 1965

Characteristic	Per cent of all MDTA public assistance trainees	Per cent of all MDTA trainees	Per cent of all MITCE trainees
Primary wage earner	86.8	60.4	96.2
Female	49.6	39.1	22.9
Family head	84.9	55.3	95.9
Five or more dependents	25.1	8.6	29.6
45 years of age and over	10.2	9.5	13.3
Unemployed 6 mths. or more [1]	59.3	29.6	13.9
Elementary school education only	20.0	14.0	39.2
Nonwhite	46.6	28.0	88.2

1. Before training.

Sources: Gerald G. Somers, "Evaluation of Work Experience and Training of Older Workers", p. 13; and MITCE client description forms.

are their family responsibilities: whether they were heads of households or the primary wage-earners in households, and the number of their dependents. The characteristics used to indicate the degree of disadvantage of trainees in the labor market follow the administrative definition of the disadvantaged adopted by the United States Department of Labor, which includes persons under 22 and over 45 years of age, nonwhites, those having completed less than 12 grades of education, those unemployed for longer than 15 weeks, and the rural poor.[42] The data in Tables 2 and 3 indicate that the average MITCE trainee had greater family responsibilities, and in most respects suffered from greater disadvantages in the labor market, than the average North Carolina or United States MDTA trainee, or the average MDTA trainee who was a welfare recipient at the time of enrolment in training.

The data from the client description forms also enable us to compare in Table 4 some indicators of the economic needs and degree of disadvantage in the labor market of MITCE trainees and the clientele of MITCE who were not trained during the project's first contract. Since it was previously observed that trainees in the MDTA-type projects studied in former benefit-cost analyses

42. See U.S., Department of Labor, Office of the Manpower Administrator, *Manpower Administration Notice No. 3-66* (Washington, D.C.: U.S. Department of Labor, 1966), pp. 1-3. (This source will subsequently be referred to in the text as the MDTA Guidelines.) The closest approximation to the concept of the "rural poor" in the available statistics for MDTA trainees appears to be the labor force status of "family farm worker" prior to enrolment in training.

Table 4: Distribution of Characteristics: MITCE Trainees,
MITCE Nontrainees and All MITCE Clients

Characteristic	Number of MITCE clients			Per cent of MITCE clients in each group		
	Trainees	Non-trainees	Total	Trainees	Non-trainees	Total
Education**	604	716	1320	100.0	100.0	100.0
0 - 8 grades	237	452	689	39.2	63.1	52.2
9 - 11 grades	214	170	384	35.4	23.7	29.1
12 grades and over	153	94	247	25.3	13.1	18.7
Sex**	619	744	1363	100.0	100.0	100.0
Male	477	455	932	77.1	61.2	68.4
Female	142	289	431	22.9	38.8	31.6
Race**	618	744	1362	100.0	100.0	100.0
Negro	438	606	1044	70.9	81.5	76.7
Indian	107	108	215	17.3	14.5	15.8
Caucasian	73	30	103	11.8	4.0	7.6
Age as of 1 Jan. 1967**	597	644	1241	100.0	100.0	100.0
Under 21 yrs.	89	72	161	14.9	11.2	13.0
21 to 33 yrs.	289	226	515	48.4	35.1	41.5
34 to 43 yrs.	131	163	294	21.9	25.3	23.7
44 yrs. and over	88	183	271	14.7	28.4	21.8
Number of Dependents	605	732	1337	100.0	100.0	100.0
None	95	93	188	15.7	12.7	14.1
1 - 3	266	298	564	44.0	40.7	42.2
4 or more	244	341	585	40.3	46.6	43.8

**   Chi-square between trainees and nontrainees significant at the .01 level.

Total and percentages are exclusive of nonascertainable responses. The list of MITCE clients comprised 619 trainees and 745 nontrainees.

Source: MT-101 client description forms.

represented the "cream" of applicants for training, it should be noted that MITCE officials also appear to have been selective in whom they admitted to training. Unlike trainees in the projects studied in former benefit-cost analyses, the average MITCE trainee was not selected on the basis of his performance on aptitude and intelligence tests.[43] However, the data in Table 4 indicate that

43.   In the initial months of operation of MITCE, some of the project's clients were admitted to institutional training courses on the basis of their performance on aptitude and intelligence tests administered by the Employment Security Commission of North Carolina. Very few of the project's clients were selected for training on this basis, however; so far as could be ascertained, only five of the trainees who were respondents in our survey of MITCE clients would have been selected for training in this manner. We will subsequently indicate why the practice of using intelligence and aptitude tests to select MITCE trainees was discontinued.

Introduction

MITCE clients were less likely to be trained if they were nonwhites, women, only had an elementary school education, or were 44 years of age or older. For these reasons, it is probable that MITCE trainees would have had higher incomes if they had not been trained than the nontrainee clientele of the project. This factor will subsequently be seen to be of some importance in our analysis of the change in earnings associated with the training of MITCE clients.

An important point brought out by both Table 2 and Table 4 is that MITCE was relatively unsuccessful in providing training for women. Fewer women were trained in proportion to their numbers in the MITCE clientele, and MITCE trained fewer women, proportionately, than the national MDTA program. It should also be noted that a greater percentage of female MITCE clients than of male MITCE clients failed to complete training courses.[44] These findings are interesting when viewed against the background of results from previous benefit-cost analyses of MDTA-type training programs; the latter also raise doubts as to whether training programs are an effective means of raising the incomes of women.[45] Such findings should be a matter of some concern in our study; one of the most significant social problems in the target areas of MITCE, as elsewhere in North Carolina, is that of the great number of low-income families headed by women. A major focus of our analysis will consequently be to investigate the effects of the training for women undertaken in the MITCE project. To this end, separate benefit-cost ratios will subsequently be estimated for the training of men and women by MITCE.

The Activities Undertaken in the MITCE Project

The MITCE project is of interest for reasons other than the characteristics of its clientele. One of the original purposes of MITCE, as stated in the project's first contract, was to demonstrate that " ... on-the-job training is a desirable and realistic training device in rural areas".[46] In fact, two-thirds of the 619 MITCE clients who were trained during the period covered by the project's first contract received on-the-job training. Nevertheless, it was not intended that such a large proportion of the project's clientele should have been trained on-the-job, and the difficulties in obtaining institutional training for MITCE clients illustrate the type of administrative regulation which prevented disadvantaged individuals from obtaining MDTA training before 1966. When the MITCE project was initiated, the North Carolina Employment Security Commission was limiting entry into MDTA institutional training courses to individuals who had completed an eighth-grade education. On this basis, a substantial proportion of MITCE clients would have been ineligible for institutional training. Tests run by the Employment Security Commission showed that an even greater proportion of MITCE clients would have been ineligible for institutional training if the entry

---

44. See the *MITCE Final Report,* p. 43.

45. See Borus, *Economic Effectiveness of Retraining the Unemployed,* p. 42, and Cain and Stromsdorfer, "Retraining in West Virginia", p. 319.

46. *MITCE Final Report,* p. 4.

qualification was interpreted to mean that the individual should have the *functional equivalent* of an eighth-grade education. The Employment Security Commission was eventually persuaded to waive this educational barrier to entry into institutional training, to stop using aptitude and intelligence tests in selecting MITCE trainees for institutional training, and to include remedial education in many of the institutional training courses arranged specifically for MITCE clients. However, only 210 MITCE clients had received institutional training by the time the project's first contract had expired, as opposed to the 400 MITCE clients for whom such training was authorized in the contract.[47]

The on-the-job and institutional training sponsored by MITCE nevertheless present some interesting contrasts. The type of on-the-job training arranged by MITCE differed in character from much of that arranged in national MDTA. MITCE did not participate in the contracts arranged at the national level with large corporations, unions and trade associations;[48] the project's on-the-job training contracts were largely concluded with small businesses. These on-the-job training contracts were written for a wide variety of occupations, and provided for training ranging in duration from 6 to 26 weeks. By way of contrast, the institutional training obtained for MITCE clients was for fewer occupations, and its duration varied from a minimum of 6 weeks to a maximum of 49 weeks. Overall, apart from the differences in the occupational skills taught in institutional and on-the-job training, and in the more immediate connection of on-the-job training with the employment of MITCE clients, it will subsequently be shown that the average on-the-job training course was shorter and less costly (to the government) than its institutional counterpart.

Another interesting aspect of the MITCE project was its extensive use of counselling services to solve problems MITCE clients encountered while in training. The writer regards one of the major findings of the project as being that the number of its clients who completed training courses was inversely related to the resources devoted to such counselling services.[49] It has long been realized that the effectiveness of training for the disadvantaged may be increased by the

---

47.   A brief account of the difficulties encountered in obtaining institutional training for MITCE clients is given in the *MITCE Final Report,* pp. 60-65.

48.   For a description of these national on-the-job training contracts, see the *Manpower Report of the President for 1969,* p. 91.

49.

The Durham Conference [in February 1966] had its ill effects as well. With a new emphasis on placements, the dropout rate rose sharply. . . . All staff members began catering to the pressures of filling quotas, and follow-ups [i.e. counselling services] became limited in the effort to get new trainees ready. When the administration realized how the production drive had affected dropouts, the Project Director instructed each area to stabilize the teams and to concentrate on following up every client properly. . . . OJT placements still rose, but OJT dropouts were held to three for the last month of the project.

MITCE Final Report, p. 50.

use of such counselling techniques.[50] But, as our analysis of MITCE will make clear, the use of such counselling techniques also substantially raises the costs of MDTA training.

Another factor which served to raise MITCE costs was the rural location of the project. Substantial costs in terms of transportation expenses and the time of MITCE personnel were involved in simply maintaining contact with MITCE clients. The MITCE clients themselves were also hampered in taking up and completing training courses because of problems in obtaining transportation and the costs of transportation when available. For example, MITCE personnel discovered one case where transportation costs were absorbing almost one-half of a trainee's take-home pay.[51] In such instances, MITCE personnel often tried to persuade clients who wished to undertake training to relocate closer to the school or job where the training was to be conducted. Such problems obviously make MDTA training projects for the rural poor a different proposition from MDTA training projects for the urban poor.

The Objectives of our Analysis of the MITCE Project

The activities undertaken in the MITCE project clearly offer a rich variety of testable hypotheses for the benefit-cost analyst. Our benefit-cost analysis of MITCE will be guided by the objectives of the Planning-Programming-Budgeting-System (PPBS), now being implemented throughout the federal government. The objective of PPBS is to indicate how specified goals can be attained in the most efficient (i.e. least-cost) manner, or alternatively, where a budget constraint limits public expenditures, to indicate how available resources can best be used to attain these goals. For reasons outlined earlier, the goal of the antipoverty program will be taken as being " ... to change people from 'poor' to 'nonpoor' *through their own efforts"*. Our principal objective will therefore be to determine the extent to which the MITCE project satisfied this distributional objective, and to determine what costs were incurred in the process. Our enquiry into the costs of training will consist of a conventional analysis of the effects of training on the allocation of resources within the economy. These "costs" could be negative, of course, if trained workers were to add more to output than the value of the resources used in their training.

It should be realized that our analysis cannot indicate whether training programs such as MITCE *should* be undertaken as a means of raising the incomes of the rural poor, since this decision requires a full knowledge of the benefits and costs of other expenditures currently being undertaken for antipoverty

---

50. On this point, see the section on "Operational Insights from E & D Projects" in the *Manpower Report of the President for 1969,* pp. 208-10.

51. See George H. Esser, Jr., "What the Rural Poor Want", mimeographed (Durham, N.C.: The North Carolina Fund, 1967), p. 6. Other instances of the transportation difficulties experienced by MITCE trainees are given in the *MITCE Final Report,* pp. 30-36.

purposes. However, given the knowledge available to us, we can indicate whether this type of training program is *likely* to be considered worth implementing as an antipoverty measure.

Our analysis will not be limited to an assessment of the overall MITCE project in terms of the distributional and efficiency criteria we have described. Our analysis also enables us to compare the relative effectiveness of institutional and on-the-job training as means of reducing poverty within the context of a rural manpower program. As noted above, we also have an interest in establishing the effects of training for male and female MITCE clients considered separately. The distributional and efficiency criteria outlined above will also be used to evaluate these aspects of the MITCE project. The benefit-cost side of our analysis can therefore be summarized as being to prepare allocative benefit-cost ratios and data on the increases in earnings associated with training for all MITCE trainees and separately for male on-the-job trainees, female on-the-job trainees, male institutional trainees and female institutional trainees.

The objectives of our benefit-cost analysis as outlined above will not provide answers to many pertinent questions arising from MITCE's training activities. Answers to these questions will, however, be sought with the aid of regression analysis of earnings data for MITCE clients. For instance, an important objective in this regression analysis will be to determine how the net earnings of MITCE clients varied with the occupation for which they were trained. Similarly, regression analysis will be used to infer whether training served to offset some of the characteristics of MITCE clients considered to convey disadvantages in the labor market. Finally, we will try to ascertain whether the transportation problems encountered by MITCE, and the different levels of counselling services provided at different times in the course of the first MITCE contract, affected the project's success in raising the earnings of its clients.

The structure of the remainder of our study can be briefly outlined. The theoretical and empirical problems encountered in benefit-cost analyses of training programs will be examined in Chapter II. The methods and findings of previous benefit-cost analyses of MDTA-type training programs will also be assessed in this chapter. A statistical analysis of the changes in earnings associated with the training of MITCE clients will be undertaken in Chapter III, based on data gathered in a survey of MITCE clients. Chapter IV will bring together the information needed to assess the distributional and allocative effects of the MITCE project. Finally, the conclusions of our study will be presented in Chapter V.

CHAPTER II

THEORETICAL AND EMPIRICAL PROBLEMS IN BENEFIT-COST ANALYSES OF TRAINING PROGRAMS

The goal of the antipoverty program was summarized in Chapter I as being " . . . to change people from 'poor' to 'nonpoor' *through their own efforts.*" The purpose of benefit-cost analysis operating within the Planning-Programming-Budgeting System is to indicate how this goal can be achieved with the least use of resources, or alternatively, if there is a budget constraint on expenditures, to indicate how the resources available to the antipoverty program can be used to make the maximum possible reduction in poverty. The function of an ex-post evaluation of any particular program undertaken in an antipoverty context, such as Manpower Improvement through Community Effort, is therefore to assess the extent to which the project met the distributional objectives of the antipoverty program, and to establish what effect the project had on the allocation of resources within the economy. This chapter will largely be devoted to analysis of the problems encountered in measuring the distributional and allocative effects of the MITCE project. A by-product of our enquiry will be a critique of the methods and findings of past benefit-cost analyses of MDTA-type training programs. The final task undertaken in this chapter will be to indicate how we plan to integrate distributional and allocative considerations in an overall evaluation of the outcome of the MITCE project.

THE DISTRIBUTIONAL EFFECTS OF TRAINING PROGRAMS

The goal of the antipoverty program − " . . . to change people from 'poor' to 'nonpoor' *through their own efforts"* − implies an aversion to reducing poverty by means of transfer payments, and a linked belief that the poor should be made better off by working. It follows that in measuring the distributional effects of the MITCE project, our primary objective is to estimate what difference training made to the ability of the project's clients to support themselves and their dependents at "adequate" income levels. Essentially this task entails estimating the effects training had on the relevant income streams of MITCE clients, and assessing the adequacy of such changes in income streams by comparisons with the income levels chosen as distinguishing the "poor" from the "nonpoor". The principal task of the first section of the present chapter will be to give a more detailed account of the steps involved in this process. The final task undertaken in this section of the chapter will be to consider whether other distributional effects of the MITCE project need be taken into account in our evaluation.

The Survey of MITCE Clients

To ascertain the difference in income streams associated with the training sponsored by MITCE, a sample survey of the trainee and nontrainee clientele of the project was undertaken. As described in Chapter I, MITCE kept records of all individuals encountered in the target areas who were eligible and available for training — regardless of whether or not these individuals were actually trained during the first MITCE contract. A stratified random sample was selected from a list of these records for individual MITCE clients. The sampling procedures employed, together with data on response variations by sampling categories, are given in Appendix A. Interviewing for the survey was conducted in the third quarter of 1967; approximately 16 months, on average, after trainees had completed their courses of instruction. The interview schedule administered to all respondents is reproduced in Appendix F. A primary purpose of the interview was to obtain an income history of the respondent for a period extending back roughly four years from the interview date. The survey data thus allow comparisons to be made between the incomes of trainees before and after training, and between the incomes of trainees and the incomes of a group of MITCE clients who were eligible to obtain training but did not in fact enter courses of instruction in the period covered by the first contract of MITCE. Either of these two comparisons could be used to draw inferences concerning the effects of training on the incomes of MITCE clients, and the grounds for choosing between the two alternatives will be discussed following a description of the particular income streams that will enter into the comparisons.

The Relevant Income Streams in an Analysis of the Distributional Benefits from MITCE

Since our objective is to establish what difference MITCE made to the ability of its clients to obtain higher incomes *by working,* the relevant income streams in our enquiry were taken to be compensation from employment and income in kind from production undertaken for home consumption. A brief outline will be given of the methods used in our survey to obtain data on these income streams of MITCE clients. Some important limitations of our data also need to be indicated.

While the procedures adopted in our survey to obtain data on the earnings of nonagricultural workers were relatively straightforward, more complex enquiries were necessary to obtain data on the compensation from employment of the many farm workers among the MITCE clientele. For instance, 44 out of a total of 444 survey respondents were self-employed as tenant farmers when they were interviewed.[1] As is well-known, the reported incomes of such self-employed workers may include returns to capital invested in their businesses and returns to the labor of unpaid family members. In an evaluation of the changes in compensation from employment associated with training, the earnings of the self-employed should be calculated net of income from these other sources. The procedures adopted to measure the net earnings from the labor of self-employed MITCE clients are described in Appendix B.

It was expected that housing provided by employers and other items of income in kind would be a significant component of the earnings of MITCE clients who were farm laborers. Survey respondents were therefore asked to estimate the value of income in kind and any other wage supplements they received as compensation from employment. In actual fact, such wage supplements were found to be comparatively unimportant as a component of the earnings of survey respondents. However, it should be noted that there are difficulties in estimating the value of some wage supplements by the method of surveying recipients of these benefits. Further details of the measurement of wage supplements in our survey, and the results of these measurements, are given in Appendix B.

It was also anticipated that income in kind from home food production would be an important item in the budgets of those MITCE clients who were farm workers. The most elaborate set of poverty lines at present available – those of Orshansky – make specific allowances for the home production of food by individuals living in rural areas.[2] A similar adjustment was undertaken in assessing the adequacy of the income levels of MITCE trainees, based on data concerning the home production of food gathered directly from respondents in our survey.

However, it is in the measurement of income in kind from nonmarket production that our estimates of the distributional benefits from training may be most deficient. Some of the training courses sponsored by MITCE – in subjects like carpentry, automotive mechanics or in textile industry trades like operating sewing machines – would seem to lend themselves to use in "do-it-yourself" activities. No attempt was made to measure any such increases in nonmarket production which might have occurred as a result of training programs. The consequences for our analysis of ignoring such distributional benefits from training would, of course, be most serious if individuals entered training courses with the principal purpose of using training to increase nonmarket production. Unfortunately, this possibility cannot be dismissed. Obviously, MDTA training courses are not intended to serve this purpose, but the conditions of eligibility for enrolment may not be sufficiently stringent to exclude individuals who lack an incentive to use the skills they acquire in employment. In this respect, one

---

1.   Five other respondents were self-employed in nonagricultural industries at the time of our survey.

2.   Mollie Orshansky, "Counting the Poor: Another Look at the Poverty Profile", *The Social Security Bulletin* 28 (Jan., 1965): 3-29.

would anticipate that the potential home uses of training might be especially attractive to women who, because of family obligations, have a low commitment to continued labor force participation. It is therefore interesting to note that some of the training courses studied by Borus were cancelled in part because the women enrolled in these courses were primarily interested in the home uses of the training.[3] It follows that we should be circumspect in assessing the distributional benefits from any training courses for women sponsored by MITCE which had potential uses in the home. Such training courses could obviously have led to distributional benefits, even if the women enrolled in these courses did not make use of the skills they acquired in subsequent employment.

Ascertaining the Difference Training Made to the Incomes of MITCE Clients

The first step in our analysis of the distributional benefits from the training sponsored by MITCE is to determine the difference training made to the income streams of MITCE clients described above. We have data on the incomes of trainees after they completed or withdrew from their courses of instruction. The additional data required in our analysis are estimates of how trainees would have fared had they not undergone training. In past benefit-cost analyses of MDTA-type training programs, two basic procedures have been used to estimate what the alternative incomes of individuals would have been in the absence of training. In one analysis — that of the Planning Research Corporation — the incomes of individuals before training were used to indicate how they would have fared without training.[4] Other benefit-cost analyses have used the incomes of "control groups" of nontrainees to indicate how trainees would have fared without training. Our survey data allow us to use either of these methods to estimate what the incomes of MITCE clients would have been in the absence of training, and the relative merits of the two procedures accordingly need to be examined.

The inference from "before-and-after" comparisons — that the incomes of individuals before training are reliable measures of how they would have fared without training — is suspect for several reasons. In the first place, trainees are often selected for participation in MDTA training programs because they are currently unemployed. Since many of the male trainees in these training programs are in age groups where nearly all members are active in the labor force, it is fallacious to assume that they would remain permanently unemployed in the absence of training. In the case of trainees in these prime labor force participation age groups, the assumption embodied in before-and-after comparisons may thus amount to ascribing permanency to what is essentially a transitory labor force status.

---

3.   See *Economic Effectiveness of Retraining the Unemployed,* p. 42.

4.   *Cost Effectiveness Analysis of On-the-Job and Institutional Training Courses,* p. 11. It should also be noted that interested executive agencies have frequently employed such "before-and-after" comparisons to illustrate the benefits from MDTA-type training programs.

Theoretical and Empirical Problems

Before-and-after comparisons of incomes can also be misleading if trainees are members of age groups where labor force participation is far from being universal. Thus one of the objectives of MDTA programs is to train large numbers of youths, again with the motive of ameliorating the high unemployment rates experienced by younger workers. However, precisely because these severe unemployment rates are associated with youth and a lack of labor market experience, the earnings and employment records of the individuals concerned can be expected to improve over time. Again, training programs which are successful in remedying a condition which is essentially one of temporary difficulty in the labor market should not necessarily be judged to have effected a permanent shift in earnings and employment opportunities. It is clear that using incomes of youths before training as an indicator of their incomes without training may again amount to ascribing permanency to transitory difficulties in the labor market.

Simple before-and-after comparisons of the incomes of trainees also ignore the effects of economic growth and of seasonal and cyclical fluctuations in economic activity. These factors affect the incomes of individuals regardless of whether they are trained or not, so that their incomes before training may not reflect what their incomes would have been without training. There appear to be good reasons for guarding against this bias of before-and-after studies in our evaluation of MITCE. The project's clients were trained in the years 1965-67. This was a period of rapid expansion in the national economy, and the rate of growth in personal income per capita was greater in North Carolina than in any other State in the Union.[5] Moreover, there is reason to believe that in these years, the growth rate in the incomes of MITCE's predominantly nonwhite clientele may have exceeded the growth rate in the incomes of other North Carolina residents. It is well established that nonwhites have made their greatest economic advances in times of economic upswings, the increase in their incomes being relatively greater than the increase in aggregate income levels in these periods.[6] It is therefore evident that there could have been a considerable improvement in the incomes of MITCE clients in the period 1965-67, regardless of whether or not they were trained by the project. In the circumstances, it would seem inadvisable to use the incomes of MITCE clients before training as an indicator of how they would have fared without training.

The approach of using control groups of nontrainees to estimate how trainees would have fared without training was therefore adopted in our analysis

---

5. Between 1965 and 1967 total personal income per capita increased by 18.3 per cent in North Carolina and by 14.3 per cent in the United States as a whole. See U. S. Department of Commerce, Office of Business Economics, *Survey of Current Business* 49 (April, 1969): 27, Table 5.

6. See W. H. Locke Anderson, "Trickling Down: The Relationship Between Economic Growth and the Extent of Poverty Among American Families", *Quarterly Journal of Economics* 78 (Nov., 1964): 511-24; James Tobin, "On Improving the Economic Status of the Negro", *Daedalus* 94 (Fall, 1965): 878-98; and Lester C. Thurow, "The Causes of Poverty", *Quarterly Journal of Economics* 71 (Feb., 1967): 39-57.

of the MITCE project. In our own study and in past benefit-cost analyses of training programs where this technique was used, the control groups of nontrainees were basically comprised of individuals who were in similar economic circumstances to trainees before training took place.

However, the method of using data on the incomes of nontrainees to estimate how trainees would have fared without training is far from being free of problems. The major difficulty is that trainees are not a random sample of the population which is available for training. In selecting trainees for MDTA programs, for instance, project officials are required to take into account the age, race, level of education and previous labor force experience of applicants. In addition, intelligence and aptitude tests — such as those in the General Aptitude Test Battery — are commonly employed in screening applicants for MDTA training programs. Of course, project officials may also be influenced by less tangible factors in selecting trainees; for instance, they may favor those applicants who display greater ambition or "drive". Indeed, since the latter applicants may be more forceful in their importunities to program officials, there may be an element of self-selection determining participation in training programs. We have to rely on statistical controls to distinguish the changes in earnings which are associated with training programs from the influences on earnings of factors which enter the selection procedures for these programs. The obvious danger in such statistical analyses of the benefits associated with training is that we may not know, or may not take into account, factors which are correlated with both earnings and participation in training.

It is not difficult to illustrate the problems which arise where variables are omitted from statistical analyses of the changes in earnings associated with training, although these variables are correlated with both earnings and participation in training. So far as can be ascertained, entry to the training programs studied in all past benefit-cost analyses was contingent on the applicant obtaining a high enough score on aptitude and intelligence tests. On the other hand, the nonapplicants for training who made up the control groups in most past analyses of training programs were not chosen on the basis of a satisfactory performance on these tests.[7] It therefore appears that, on average, trainees were

---

7.   In all of the studies of training programs in West Virginia, the nonapplicant control group was comprised of a random sample of nontrainees who were represented in the files of the local employment services and who were unemployed immediately prior to the commencement of the training programs. See Somers and Stromsdorfer, "Benefit-Cost Analysis of Manpower Retraining", p. 173; Cain and Stromsdorfer, "Retraining in West Virginia", p. 302; Stromsdorfer, "Determinants of Economic Success in Retraining", pp. 141-42. Page's nontrainee control group " . . . was comprised of a random sample of individuals in the central claims file of the Bureau of Employment Security having six characteristics similar to those of trainees". See his "Retraining under the Manpower Development Act", p. 263.

Of all previous analyses which employed control groups to estimate the benefits from training, only the study by Borus does not rely on comparisons between the incomes of trainees and nonapplicants for training. In calculating the private returns from training, Borus employed control groups of individuals who satisfied the General Aptitude Test Battery requirements for entry into training. In estimating the returns to society from training no control group was necessary in Borus' study, in view of his contention that the entire earnings of trainees represented benefits to society. See *Economic Effectiveness of Retraining the Unemployed*, chaps. I and II.

more able and intelligent than the nonapplicants for training with whom they were compared in previous studies of training programs. However, no direct statistical controls were introduced into the analyses of previous studies to allow for this difference in the "quality" of trainees and nonapplicants for training. The problem in interpreting the findings of these studies should thus be evident. While all of these analyses found that the incomes of trained workers were higher than those of nonapplicants for training, there is no way of knowing whether this difference in incomes was attributable to the training programs or to the difference in the levels of ability and intelligence between trainees and nonapplicants for training.

As noted in Chapter I, MITCE trainees were not selected on the basis of their performance on aptitude and intelligence tests. However, it was also shown in Chapter I that trainees were far from being a random sample of the MITCE clientele which was eligible and available for training, and there is little doubt that MITCE clients who were trained would have had higher incomes without training than the nontrainee clientele of the project. For instance, our comparisons of a few of the characteristics of trainees and nontrainees in Chapter I indicated that MITCE clients were less likely to be trainees if they were nonwhites, women, 44 years of age or older, or had only an elementary school education. Obviously, there may have been other systematic differences in the characteristics of trainees and nontrainees which would have led to differences in their incomes even if training had never taken place. Extensive efforts were therefore made in our survey of MITCE clients to obtain information on the characteristics of individuals which were expected to have an influence on their income levels. These characteristics will be used as independent variables in the regression analysis which will be undertaken in Chapter III to determine the distributional benefits associated with the training sponsored by MITCE.

The Use of Poverty Income Levels in Assessing the Distributional Benefits of the MITCE Project

Once we have estimated the difference made by training to the incomes of MITCE clients, the next step in our analysis is to assess the effectiveness of training in reducing poverty. While several estimates of the income levels which distinguish the "poor" from the "nonpoor" are available, our study will primarily rely on the poverty lines developed by Orshansky and used by many executive agencies. However, it was also felt that there would be advantages in taking a more pragmatic approach to the problem of defining poverty income lines, in view of the prevailing differences of opinion on the methodology of constructing such lines. Consequently, the poverty income levels developed by authors other than Orshansky will also be used to illustrate the distributional benefits from the MITCE project.

The issues involved in *choosing* poverty lines are nevertheless distinct from the issues involved in *using* poverty lines to assess the adequacy of antipoverty programs. The least complicated criterion of the effectiveness of antipoverty programs is whether they are successful in raising the income levels of their clients above poverty lines. This line-crossing standard has the virtues of being easy to understand and to apply, and will be used in our study. However, the line-crossing criterion alone is an inadequate test of the effectiveness of antipoverty measures, and will be supplemented in our analysis by other considerations.

One of the more obvious defects of the line-crossing standard is that it attributes no value to programs which leave the poor better off, although failing to raise their incomes above the poverty line. Other criteria for assessing the effectiveness of antipoverty measures have been proposed which do take account of such intramarginal changes in the incomes of the poor. For instance, Lampman has introduced the concept of the "poverty income gap" – or the dollar amount by which the incomes of the poor fall short of the poverty line. Lampman suggests that the goals of the antipoverty program should be to both close the poverty income gap and move people across the poverty line.[8]

However, even the Lampman criteria fail to reflect adequately the objectives of the antipoverty program. For instance, it is reasonable to suppose that a corollary to our concern for reducing poverty is a preference for ameliorating the condition of those people at the most severe levels of poverty. The Lampman criteria fail to reflect this concern; for instance, any amount of income relief to families living at the most severe levels of poverty has the same value in reducing the poverty income gap as an equal amount of income relief to families who, while still poor, are at slightly higher income levels.

An appealing method of dealing with income gains short of the poverty line is that proposed by Ribich; namely to weight these gains according to the income ranges of the people affected by antipoverty programs. In Ribich's proposal, increases in the incomes of families or individuals in the neighborhood of the poverty line would be counted at their full dollar value, or in other words would receive a weight of unity. The further family or individual income levels were below the poverty line, the greater would be the weight assigned to any increases in their incomes.[9]

Of course, any scheme for weighting the distributional benefits from antipoverty programs immediately encounters the problem of dealing with increases in incomes above the poverty line. Another obvious defect of the line-crossing or Lampman criteria for evaluating the success of antipoverty programs is that they imply a lack of concern for the welfare of the low-income population once the incomes of the latter rise above the poverty line. Under either the criterion of reducing the poverty income gap, or that of moving

---

8. Robert J. Lampman, "Approaches to the Reduction of Poverty", *American Economic Review* 55 (May, 1965): 523.

9. *Education and Poverty*, p. 30.

people across the poverty line, income gains above the poverty line are assumed to have no value. However, it is clear that we should not be indifferent to income gains above the poverty line. For instance, an antipoverty program which raised a family's income considerably above the poverty line would without doubt be preferred to an equally costly program which just managed to raise the same family's income above the poverty line.

Another merit of Ribich's criteria for evaluating antipoverty measures is that they allow us to indicate our preference for the first program outcome in the above illustration. Ribich suggests that a second and higher poverty line should be determined which would indicate an upper limit to society's willingness to raise the incomes of the poor. The introduction of the second poverty line permits a symmetrical resolution to the problem of weighting income gains attributable to antipoverty measures. Income gains above the second poverty line would receive zero weight in assessments of antipoverty programs, since by definition society is no longer interested in spending money to benefit individuals in this income range. On the other hand, income gains between the upper and lower poverty lines would receive weights graduated from zero to unity.[10]

There are practical difficulties in applying all of the criteria proposed by Ribich for assessing the effectiveness of antipoverty programs.[11] Nevertheless, even a rough application of Ribich's criteria would appear to be superior to use of the "line-crossing" or Lampman standards for evaluating the effectiveness of antipoverty measures, and this step will accordingly be undertaken in our analysis of the MITCE project.

Other Distributional Effects of the MITCE Project

To this point, our analysis has been concerned with the distributional effects of *expenditures* incurred in the MITCE project. Logically, an interest in the distributional effects of public expenditures should be complemented by an equal interest in the distributional implications of the *financing* of these expenditures. However, Musgrave has suggested that the question of the distributional effects of the financing mechanism " ... may be bypassed by ranking alternative public investments, while holding the source of finance constant, so that the distributional effects on the revenue side are the same".[12] Since the stratagem suggested by Musgrave provides a convenient rationale for focusing our analysis on the effects of MITCE expenditures, it was accordingly adopted in the present study. However, it is recognized that the distributional

---

10. *Ibid.*, pp. 29-30.

11. For instance, Ribich believes that both of the poverty lines he advocates should be determined by public consensus, and we obviously lack information of this kind. See *Education and Poverty*, pp. 25-27.

12. Richard A. Musgrave, "Cost-Benefit Analysis and the Theory of Public Finance", *Journal of Economic Literature* 7 (Sept., 1969): 805.

implications of government revenues would need to be taken into account if the question at issue were the optimum size of government expenditures in the absence of a budget constraint.[13]

THE ALLOCATIVE EFFECTS OF TRAINING

Until comparatively recent years, benefit-cost analysts have made a rigid distinction between questions of the distributional equity of public expenditures and the allocative efficiency of these expenditures, and empirical analysis has concentrated on determining whether particular programs are likely to be allocatively efficient. A program is only judged to improve the allocation of resources if it increases *total* opportunities for production and consumption within the economy; in other words, if its "real" benefits exceed its "real" costs. Any "pecuniary" effects of public expenditures − those which alter the distribution of income without changing total opportunities for production or consumption − are, of course, ignored in assessing the allocative efficiency of programs.[14] Our analysis of the allocative efficiency of the MITCE project will follow this established practice. Our immediate task is therefore to outline the various kinds of real benefits and costs that can result from training programs, and to indicate how we propose to measure these real effects in our evaluation of the MITCE project.

THE REAL BENEFITS FROM TRAINING

The distribution over time of possible real benefits from training programs adds complexity to assessment of the allocative effects of the MITCE project. Training programs, like other investments in human capital, may continue to yield real benefits for many years after the costs of instruction have been incurred. For instance, training may increase the productivity of individuals over the remainder of their working lifetimes. To find what effects the MITCE project had on the allocation of resources within the economy, we therefore have to estimate the discounted value of all future benefits from training at the time the costs of training were incurred. The data from our survey of MITCE clients will be used to estimate the value of such future streams of allocative benefits from training undertaken in the MITCE project. Accordingly, in the present section of this chapter, we need to establish criteria for judging whether there were any allocative benefits from training in the survey period.

---

13. *Ibid.*

14. See for example, A. R. Prest and R. Turvey, "Cost-Benefit Analysis: A Survey", *The Economic Journal* 75 (Dec., 1965): 688; and Burton A. Weisbrod, "Concepts of Costs and Benefits", in *Problems in Public Expenditure Analysis*, ed. Samuel B. Chase, Jr. (Washington, D.C.: The Brookings Institution, 1968), pp. 257-62.

Theoretical and Empirical Problems

Increases in Productivity Associated with Training Programs

Since the primary purpose of MDTA training is to allow workers to acquire vocational skills, it is to be expected that the principal real benefits from training would take the form of increases in the productivity of workers. As noted in our examination of the possible distributional benefits from training, the data from our survey of MITCE clients do not allow us to measure any increases in nonmarket output which may well be associated with training. For this reason, it is valid to assume that our estimates of both the allocative and distributional returns from training will be biased downward. However, we can use the data on earnings from our survey of MITCE clients to infer whether training led to increases in that part of the output of workers which is priced in the market. The classic exposition of such allocative effects of on-the-job training has been given by Becker.[15] The principles underlying Becker's analysis of on-the-job training can also be extended to analysis of the allocative effects of the institutional training undertaken in MDTA programs, and indeed to analysis of the allocative effects of schooling in general. While our immediate concern is with the implications of Becker's analysis for estimates of the allocative benefits from training, a brief description of his entire model will be presented, in view of its equally important implications for analysis of the allocative costs of training.

Becker's model of the allocative effects of on-the-job training is set in the abstract framework of a world of perfectly competitive markets. The most important analytical distinction made by Becker is between "general" and "specific" training: the former being useful to many firms; the latter being useful only to the firm providing the training. Since general training is useful to many firms, and since profit-maximizing employers in perfectly competitive markets will hire labor up to the point where the value of its marginal product is equal to its wage, it follows that we can measure the contribution training makes to the productivity of workers by finding what difference training makes to their earnings before taxes.

The costs of general on-the-job training in Becker's model are also derived by making use of data on the earnings of workers. Since firms cannot appropriate any of the returns from general on-the-job training, they will only provide this type of instruction if they are fully reimbursed for its costs. Accordingly, workers will pay for general on-the-job training by accepting wages during the period of instruction which are below those which they could obtain from other employers.

Becker suggests that there is no sharp theoretical distinction between schooling and general on-the-job training, and that schools should simply be treated as institutions which specialize in the "business" of training. Direct outlays for items like tuition should of course be added to the forgone earnings

---

15. Gary S. Becker, *Human Capital* (New York: National Bureau of Economic Research, 1964), chap. II.

of students in estimating the opportunity costs of schooling; otherwise, the allocative effects of schooling would be derived on the principles outlined in Becker's model of the allocative effects of general on-the-job training.

On the other hand, Becker suggests that the costs of training which is useful only to the firm providing the training, and the returns from such specific training, will be shared between workers and firms. In the period during which specific training is undertaken, the firm may absorb some of the costs of training by paying workers wages that are higher than the actual value of their marginal products. But the promise of future wage increases may also induce workers to bear some of the costs of specific training, by accepting wages during the period of instruction which are lower than those they could receive elsewhere in the economy. After specific training is completed, the firm will attempt to recoup any costs it bears for specific training by paying workers wages that are less than the value of their marginal products, but more than the wages they could receive from other employers.

While Becker's distinction between general and specific training is of considerable analytical value, in practice it seems likely that most on-the-job training would combine both elements of instruction. This point is important because it is impossible in the present study to measure any of the returns from specific training which accrue to firms. Since our data source is a cross-section survey of the earnings of MITCE clients, our measure of the allocative returns from training can only reflect the returns from general on-the-job training and any of the returns from specific on-the-job training which accrue to workers. To be consistent, it follows that we should also exclude any of the costs of specific training which are borne by firms in estimating the allocative effects of the training sponsored by the MITCE project.[16]

While Becker's analysis demonstrates that on-the-job training may lead to differences between the wages and the productivity of workers even in a hypothetical world of perfectly competitive markets, such differences may of course also be caused by imperfections in real world markets. However, in order to show that market imperfections invalidate the assumption that earnings differentials associated with past investments in human capital reflect productivity differentials among workers, it would seem necessary to demonstrate that market imperfections are systematically related to these investments. A number of critics have in fact challenged estimates of the social

---

16. This procedure also has the incidental advantage of avoiding the difficult problems encountered in identifying the costs of specific training which are borne by firms. According to Mincer,

> Even if all costs of training were borne by firms, so that they would also pay all the foregone earnings of workers, only a fraction of costs would be revealed by accounting data. I conclude that an attempt to gauge costs of on-the-job training in the economy by accounting data of firms, even if they were made available, would lead to severe underestimates.

Jacob Mincer, "On-the-Job Training: Costs, Returns, and Implications", *Journal of Political Economy* 70 (Supplement, Oct., 1962): 52.

returns from education on the grounds that earnings differentials associated with education may reflect employer discrimination in favor of more educated workers rather than productivity differentials among members of the labor force. It is also possible that employer and official discrimination in favor of MDTA trainees may lead to increases in their earnings which exaggerate the contribution training makes to their productivity. These hypotheses will now be examined.

Possible Pecuniary Effects of Education and Training Programs

Although most empirical investigations of the returns to investments in human capital have equated the productivity of workers with their annual earnings, several writers have taken the position that estimates of the returns to education should not reflect differences in the rates of employment of workers. Thus Weisbrod, together with Morgan and his coauthors, have argued that the inverse relationship between the unemployment rates and educational attainments of workers should be attributed to inadequate aggregate demand in the economy, and hence to inadequate macroeconomic policies.[17] In examining this argument, it is necessary to ask why inadequate aggregate demand would lead firms to employ the more highly educated rather than the less highly educated. However, a means of reconciling the hypothesis that unemployment is caused by inadequate aggregate demand with the observed inverse relationship between the unemployment rates and levels of education of workers has been

---

17. Weisbrod puts this point of view concisely:

> It seems to me analytically unwise to mix study of the allocative efficiency of additional expenditures on education with study of the efficiency of monetary and fiscal policy in maintaining full employment. I would like to urge that in looking at the question of whether to invest more in education, we consider what students could earn and produce, not what they might actually earn or produce, as affected by unemployment.

Burton A. Weisbrod, "Education and Investment in Human Capital", p. 123. James Morgan and Martin David oppose the use of annual earnings in measuring the returns to education on more broad grounds:

> Annual money earnings indicate not only productivity but also reflect the unwanted unemployment of the less educated, and the desired extra leisure that can be afforded by those with more education. We should not attribute to education differences which result from the failure to preserve full employment, nor should we undervalue extra education because some of its benefit is taken in longer vacations or shorter hours.

"Education and Income", *Quarterly Journal of Economics* 77 (Aug., 1963): 423. James Morgan and Ismail Sirageldin present essentially similar arguments against the use of annual earnings in measuring the allocative effects of education, but also note that " . . . if one is interested in social return, it can be argued that differential unemployment should be charged to inadequate national fiscal and monetary policy, not to differentials in education". "A Note on the Quality Dimension of Education", *Journal of Political Economy* 76 (Sept., 1968): 1069-70.

provided by those writers who believe that employers use education as a screening device in hiring workers.[18]

Proponents of the view that education is used as a screening device by employers point out that where there are many applicants for job openings, the task of selecting employees can be an expensive process unless some job applicants are rejected by rules of thumb. It is argued that ranking job applicants on the basis of their educational attainments is one such rule that can be used to reduce hiring costs considerably. Paradoxically, this hypothesis implies that an adequate performance can be obtained in many occupations from persons having considerably different levels of education. However, it is contended that employers may have good reasons for using educational attainments as a screening device, even if the knowledge acquired in education is largely irrelevant to a worker's job functions. Since more able individuals tend to stay in school longer, employers may be justified in using the levels of education of job applicants as surrogate measures of their ability. In addition, educational qualifications could well be indicators of other traits which are considered desirable in employees. One of the functions of the schooling system may be to inculcate industrial disciplines in individuals, and employers may regard the completion of educational programs as an indication that individuals have absorbed these disciplines. In other words, diplomas or degrees may function as "certificates of reliability", indicating that their holders have demonstrated the competence or persistence to complete a task and to get along with peers and superiors in the process. For this reason, individuals could very well obtain a "bonus for graduation" in the job market.[19]

Of course, some of the personality traits described above may lead to real differences in the productivity of persons with differing levels of education, even if the actual knowledge acquired in education is of no value in performing

---

18. Two of the best discussions of the use of education as a screening device occur in reviews of Becker's *Human Capital:* Albert Rees, *American Economic Review* 55 (Sept. 1965): 959-60, and Robert M. Solow, *Journal of Political Economy* 73 (Oct., 1965): 552-53. See also Rudolph C. Blitz, "The Nation's Educational Outlay", in U.S., Department of Health, Education and Welfare, Office of Education, *Economics of Higher Education,* ed. Selma J. Mushkin (Washington, D.C.: Government Printing Office, 1962), p. 155; Hansen, Weisbrod and Scanlon, "Schooling and Earnings of Low Achievers", pp. 415-16; John Keats, *The Sheepskin Psychosis* (Philadelphia: Lippincott, 1965); Fritz Machlup, *The Production and Distribution of Knowledge in the United States* (Princeton, N.J.: Princeton University Press, 1962), pp. 114-15; Michael K. Taussig, "An Economic Analysis of Vocational Education in the New York City High Schools", *Journal of Human Resources* 3 (Supplement, 1968): 72.

19. It has often been found that the returns from completing the terminal years of educational programs are higher than those from completing the initial years of the same programs. For instance, Hanoch's estimates of rates of return to education show that white college graduates in the North, white college and high school graduates in the South, and nonwhite high school graduates in the South all benefit from such "sheepskin effects". The rates of return referred to are unadjusted for ability differentials. See "An Economic Analysis of Earnings and Schooling", p. 322. The hypothesis outlined in the text has been advanced as a reason for the existence of these "sheepskin effects". See Rees, "Review of *Human Capital*", p. 959.

specific job functions. Thus at full employment, firms may well be justified in paying more educated workers higher wages for performing the same tasks as less educated workers. But in a slack labor market, the use of education as a screening device implies that the better educated are considered employable *at the expense* of their less educated counterparts, and consequently that annual earnings differentials exaggerate the productivity differentials among workers of different educational levels. Such transfer payments from the less educated to the more educated should obviously not be confused with the real benefits from investments in human capital.

General education may not be the only type of schooling which could be used as a screening device by employers; some analysts have maintained that employers accept completion of training programs as evidence that job applicants have demonstrated above average motivation and ability.[20] Thus in a slack labor market, it is clear that some of the returns from completing training programs may also represent pecuniary effects from the point of view of society.[21]

Discrimination on the part of employers may not be the only reason why increases in employment associated with the completion of training programs might represent pecuniary effects from the point of view of society; the job-placement activities of training program officials could have the same effect.

---

20. In their analysis of West Virginia training programs, Somers and Stromsdorfer note that,

> Even when they were not hired in occupations for which they were trained, the training may have had a crucial influence on the trainees' future employment success. They gained some versatility, and many employers preferred them because these workers had demonstrated sufficient ambition and sense of discipline to enter and complete a training course.

"Benefit-Cost Analysis of Manpower Retraining", p. 175. Borus also claims that,

> ... the occupational mobility and motivation demonstrated by the workers in participating in retraining encouraged employers to hire retrainees for non-retraining-related occupations.

Economic Effectiveness of Retraining the Unemployed, p. 10. Solie reports the same phenomenon in the Tennessee training programs he studied:

> Although 35 percent of those who obtained jobs did not make direct use of their training, it cannot be concluded that they did not benefit from the training program. ... Many employers, even though they had no need for the specific skills acquired in training, viewed the training program as a good screening device, since by completing the program the completes had exhibited both ability and motivation.

"Employment Effects of Retraining the Unemployed", p. 214.

21. The use of educational or training program diplomas as screening devices by employers raises issues other than those associated with redistribution of income in slack labor markets. If the diplomas serve primarily as indicators of personality traits which are useful in employment, perhaps greater attention should be paid to the influence of schooling or training programs in developing these traits. On the other hand, if the diplomas simply function as certificates of the inherent personality traits of the individual, it might well be argued that there are less costly and more efficient ways of obtaining this information than by schooling or training programs.

Thus MITCE officials made special efforts to find employment for trainees who completed their courses of instruction, as did the officials in charge of the training programs studied in past benefit-cost analyses.[22] Neither in the MITCE project nor in the training programs studied in past analyses were corresponding efforts made to find employment for dropouts from training programs or for the nontrainees comprising the control groups in most studies. In the circumstances, the analyst is faced with the difficult task of determining whether any increases in employment associated with the completion of these training programs are attributable to the training itself or to the job-placement activities of training program officials.

Two factors would seem to have an important bearing on the consequences for evaluations of training programs of employer and official discrimination in favor of training completors. In the first place, the effects of official discrimination in favor of training completors are likely to decline with the passage of time and normal job-turnover on the part of trainees and nontrainees. Thus, the longer the interval between the completion of courses of instruction and observation of the earnings of trainees and nontrainees, the less important are the job-placement activities of training program officials likely to be. However, the survey periods for which data were collected on the earnings of trainees and control groups in the present and past analyses of training programs were comparatively short — varying in duration from a minimum of 12 months to a maximum of 27 months after trainees completed their courses of instruction.[23] In these relatively brief survey periods, it is only to be expected that efforts made to find jobs for completors of training programs would lead

---

22. Section 202 of the Manpower Development and Training Act in fact requires program officials to make efforts to place trainees who complete courses of instruction. Several authors of previous studies of training programs have acknowledged the importance of the job-placement activities that were made on behalf of training completors in the programs they studied. See Borus, *The Economic Effectiveness of Retraining the Unemployed,* p. 10, Cain and Stromsdorfer, "Retraining in West Virginia", pp. 322-23.

In the MITCE Project, it was unnecessary to find jobs for workers who completed on-the-job training courses, since in the normal course of events, these trainees continued to be employed by the firms which sponsored their training. Accordingly, some of these on-the-job trainees were likely to have uninterrupted employment records throughout the entire period after training for which earnings and employment data were gathered in our survey of MITCE clients. For this reason, the employment records of on-the-job training completors are likely to be better in the survey period than those of institutional training completors. According to MITCE officials, many institutional trainees were not able to enter employment immediately after completing their courses of instruction.

23. As noted earlier, the survey of MITCE clients provides us with earnings data for a period averaging 16 months after trainees completed their courses of instruction. Former analyses of training programs by both Borus and the Planning Research Corporation were based on survey periods of a year, and the various studies of West Virginia training programs made use of survey periods ranging from 18 to 27 months in duration. See Borus, *Economic Effectiveness of Retraining the Unemployed,* pp. 18-20; Planning Research Corporation, *Cost-Effectiveness Analysis of On-the-Job and Institutional Training Courses,* p. 11; Cain and Stromsdorfer, "Retraining in West Virginia", p. 308; Somers and Stromsdorfer, "Benefit-Cost Analysis of Manpower Retraining", pp. 178-79; Stromsdorfer, "Determinants of Economic Success in Retraining the Unemployed", p. 141.

their employment records to be better than those of dropouts from training programs or nontrainee members of control groups.

The importance of employer or official discrimination in favor of training program completors would also vary with the levels of unemployment obtaining in the survey periods of analyses of training programs. In this respect, there were marked differences in the labor market conditions prevailing during the survey period of our study of the MITCE project, and in the labor market conditions prevailing during the survey periods of most past analyses of training programs. In the period 1965-67, when MITCE clients were trained and were interviewed in our survey, the average unemployment rate in North Carolina was 3.6 per cent of the labor force.[24] By way of contrast, most of the training programs studied in former benefit-cost analyses took place in the early 1960's, when unemployment was at far higher levels.[25] In the slack labor markets characteristic of the survey periods of past analyses of training programs, "sheepskin effects" and the job-placement activities of training program officials could have led to marked increases in the employment of completors of training programs.

While deficient aggregate demand in the economy could explain why some of the employment "benefits" of education and training programs might be pecuniary effects, there are other explanations of the inverse relationship between the unemployment rates and skill or educational levels of workers. In particular, the assumption underlying the Manpower Development and Training Act is that such differences in unemployment rates may reflect persistent imbalances between the supply of skills and the demand for skills in labor markets.[26] The Act proposes that equilibrium in these labor markets should be

---

24.   U. S., Department of Labor, *1969 Statistics on Manpower: A Supplement to the Manpower Report of the President* (Washington, D.C.: Government Printing Office, 1969), p. 61.

25.   In the various studies of West Virginia programs, training and the survey of trainees took place in the period 1961-64. Unemployment rates in the counties where training was conducted ranged from 6.0 per cent to 23.5 per cent in this period. See Gibbard and Somers, "Government Retraining in West Virginia", p. 124. Training and the survey of trainees in the Connecticut programs studied by Borus took place in the years 1961-63. Unemployment rates in the localities where training was conducted ranged from 3 per cent to 12 per cent in this period. See *Economic Effectiveness of Retraining the Unemployed*, p. 104. Page indicates that the workers in the Massachusetts programs he studied were trained in the years 1958-61. The average unemployment rate in Massachusetts in this period was 5.9 per cent. See "Retraining under the Manpower Development Act", p. 262, and *1969 Statistics on Manpower*, p. 61. However, the benefit-cost analysis of national MDTA training by the Planning Research Corporation covers a time period which overlaps that of our own study of MITCE clients. The training courses studied by the Planning Research Corporation took place in the years 1963-65, when the average unemployment rate in the U.S. was 5.1 per cent. See *Cost-Effectiveness Analysis of On-the-Job Training and Institutional Training Courses*, p. 4, and *1969 Statistics on Manpower*, p. 16.

26.   Thus according to Section 101 of the Manpower Development and Training Act,

The Congress finds . . . that even in periods of high unemployment, many employment opportunities remain unfilled because of the shortage of qualified personnel; and that it is in the national interest that current and prospective manpower shortages be identified and that persons who can be qualified for these positions through education and training be sought out and trained as quickly as is reasonably possible. . . .

attained not by increasing aggregate *demand,* but by using training programs to change the skill composition of the labor *supply.*

The fact that increases in employment associated with the completion of training programs could represent either pecuniary benefits to trainees or genuine reductions in structural unemployment therefore poses a dilemma for analyses of the allocative effects of training programs. However, various methods of distinguishing between the real and pecuniary employment effects of training programs have been proposed in the literature, and their relative merits will now be considered.

The "Requirements" Approach to Distinguishing Between the Pecuniary and Real Effects of Training Programs

A possible means of establishing whether training reduces unemployment by altering the skill composition of the labor supply is to determine whether training satisfies a *requirement* for employment in occupations where there are excess demands for labor. Considerations of this type underlie the benefit-cost analyses of training programs by Borus and Page. The assumptions made in these studies require close examination, because they lead both authors to make significant departures from the procedures usually adopted in estimating the allocative benefits from investments in human capital.

The innovations in the study by Borus are based on two assumptions.[27] In the first place, Borus maintains that there was an inadequate supply of skilled labor in the occupations for which training took place, and that the jobs obtained by workers who used skills taught in training courses would otherwise have been unfilled. Secondly, Borus assumes that trainees were either unemployed before training or had jobs in which they could easily be replaced by unskilled workers. These assumptions lead Borus to reject the usual practice of regarding the *increases* in earnings of trainees as representing increases in their productivity. Borus argues that the *entire* earnings of workers who used their training represented the increase in output resulting from training programs, since not only were the earnings of these workers raised as a result of training, but formerly unemployed members of the labor force were able to obtain any jobs these trainees held before training. In addition, Borus argues that there were no allocative benefits from training workers who did not proceed to use skills taught in training courses, since these trainees were simply depriving unskilled workers of jobs.

In many respects, the assumptions made by Page in his analysis of Massachusetts training programs are similar to the assumptions made by Borus. Thus Page argues that there was excess demand for workers in the occupations for which training took place, and considers that training only led to allocative

---

27. The methodology used by Borus is given on pp. 40-45 of *Economic Effectiveness of Retraining the Unemployed.*

benefits where workers completed their courses of instruction and "were employed in the field for which they were trained". However, Page's calculation of the allocative benefits from training is "conventional" in the sense that he regards the *increase* in the earnings of training completors who were employed in fields related to their training as representing the change in output associated with training programs.[28]

The difficulties in accepting the arguments of Borus and Page stem partly from other information supplied in their studies. It is not evident, for instance, that there was excess demand for workers in the occupations for which training took place in the Massachusetts programs. Thus Page reports, "The primary reason (33 per cent) given by the trainees for not finding a job related to their training was the absence of vacancies, as evidenced by unsuccessful applications to different firms."[29] In any event, it does not follow that workers who satisfied Page's criterion — i.e., "were employed in the field for which they were trained" — obtained jobs which were unavailable to workers who did not participate in training programs. Nor is it apparent that workers found by Borus to be using their training in subsequent employment were obtaining jobs which were unavailable to workers who were not trained. Thus, 7 per cent of the respondents in Borus' survey who said they were using skills taught in training courses also asserted that they could have obtained their jobs without training. What is more, Borus remarks that these trainees " ... were probably correct in their claim because 19 per cent of the workers in the sample who withdrew from retraining or refused retraining were subsequently placed in jobs which used skills taught in the retraining courses".[30]

While the information supplied by sample members in the Borus and Page studies therefore does not appear to warrant the assumption that workers required their MDTA training to obtain employment in "skill-shortage" occupations, there is some doubt as to how much weight should be attached to the opinion of trainees and nontrainees on this issue.[31] Unfortunately, it appears that little is to be gained by using the estimates of independent observers to ascertain whether workers required the training provided by MDTA programs to obtain employment in specific occupations, except in cases where such

---

28. "Retraining under the Manpower Development Act", pp. 262-65.

29. *Ibid.*, p. 262.

30. *Economic Effectiveness of Retraining the Unemployed*, p. 26.

31. Other studies of vocational training have shown that the practice of asking trainees to assess the value of their training in jobs they subsequently obtained is of dubious value. Thus Taussig reports that roughly three-quarters of all 1965 vocational high school graduates in New York City considered that they were employed in an "occupation related to [their] school program". Yet expert opinion belies the assumption that the training obtained by graduates of these vocational training programs is relevant to their subsequent employment. See "An Economic Analysis of Vocational Education in the New York City High Schools", p. 74. The problems involved in trainee evaluation of the relevance of their instruction have also been stressed by Einar Hardin. See his "Benefit-Cost Analyses of Occupational Training Programs", in *Cost-Benefit Analysis of Manpower Policies,* ed. G. G. Somers and W. D. Wood (Kingston, Ont.: Industrial Relations Centre, Queen's University, 1969), p. 106.

requirements happen to be specified by the state, or by the fiats of professional associations or unions.[32] Where the latter "requirements" do not exist, parallel endeavours to estimate the educational requirements of occupations encounter the difficulty of explaining why there are wide variations in the years of schooling of members of most occupations. One explanation that has been advanced for the latter phenomenon is that formal education, on-the-job training, and experience are good substitutes for the purpose of acquiring competence in many skills.[33] If a high degree of such substitution is possible in the formation of skills, of course, the search for the educational or training requirements of occupations becomes a futile exercise.

There is an additional reason for rejecting the criteria adopted by Borus and Page in determining whether training led to allocative benefits. These authors assume that training only led to increases in output where trainees used skills learned in training courses, or worked in fields related to their training. However, training could well increase the productivity of workers in ways which are completely unrelated to the occupational value of the subject matter taught in training courses. In this respect, vocational training may share some of the attributes of nonvocational schooling, whose economic value is even less likely to lie in any occupational skills imparted by the schools. For instance, MITCE personnel placed considerable emphasis on accustoming their predominantly

---

32. Some of the problems encountered in estimating the skill requirements of jobs can be illustrated from one of the most exhaustive studies in this field: U.S., Department of Labor, Bureau of Employment Security, *Estimates of Worker Traits Requirements for 4000 Jobs* (Washington, D.C.: Government Printing Office, 1956). The basis for classification in the BES study is the amount of general educational development (GED) and specific vocational preparation (SVP) " . . . necessary for a worker to have acquired the knowledge and abilities essential for average performance in a specific job". *(Ibid.*, p. v.). The data in this study have subsequently been reworked by Eckaus and Scoville to obtain estimates of educational and training requirements for workers classified by Census of Population industries and occupations: R. S. Eckaus, "Economic Criteria for Education and Training", *Review of Economics and Statistics* 46 (May, 1964): 181-90, and James G. Scoville, "Education and Training Requirements for Occupations", *Review of Economics and Statistics* 48 (Nov., 1966): 387-94. However, Scoville reveals several gross shortcomings in the BES estimates, of which perhaps the most serious occurs in the measurement of the vocational training required for jobs:

> In measuring GED the origin of the measuring rod is fairly clear – the commencement of formal education. With SVP the answer to the question of a starting point is not so evident. . . . At no point in the BES publication are these problems met squarely. The "seat of the pants" estimating procedure implied by that publication is hardly reassuring.

Nor are the BES estimates of the educational requirements of jobs free from problems; according to Scoville, some of these estimates are " . . . almost impossible to comprehend". Moreover, Scoville presents the interesting finding that in 1960, 28 per cent of the labor force was in occupations where the median level of education fell short of that estimated as being " . . . essential for average performance in a specific job". As Scoville rightly remarks, this finding " . . . must call either the basic data or our estimating procedure into question". See "Education and Training Requirements for Occupations", pp. 391-92.

33. A summary of the evidence on variations of years of schooling among members of particular occupations, and on the substitutability of schooling, on-the-job training and experience in the formation of skills, is given by Samuel Bowles in *Planning Educational Systems for Economic Growth* (Cambridge, Mass.: Harvard University Press, 1969), pp. 50-54.

rural clientele to the discipline and personal habits involved in successfully holding down jobs in the nonagricultural sector of the economy.[34] It has been surmised that the principal economic contribution of the lower levels of education may consist in inculcating similar industrial disciplines.[35] It is also possible that training programs, like schooling, may increase the productivity of workers through other indirect routes.[36] For these reasons, one cannot assume that training only increases the productivity of workers who proceed to use the vocational subject matter taught in training courses.

Indeed, it would seem advisable in benefit-cost analyses of training programs to avoid making any prior assumptions as to whether or not training increases the productivity of specific categories of workers. Page and Borus were not the only authors of past analyses who made assumptions of this kind. Thus the benefit-cost ratios in the various analyses of West Virginia training programs, as well as that produced by Page, were constructed on the principles that there were no allocative benefits from training dropouts from training courses, and that the costs of training dropouts were simply an unavoidable cost of producing graduates from these courses.[37] These assumptions are far from being inconsequential, in view of the large number of dropouts from these programs and from MDTA training in general.[38] Nor is it clear why the authors of these

---

34. See the *MITCE Final Report*, p. 34.

35. According to Bowles,

   It may not be an exaggeration to suggest that from the employer's standpoint, the main function of primary education is not to enlighten or to impart particular job skills, but to teach youth to come on time, to adjust to boring routine, and to take orders from someone outside the family or traditional system of authority. . . . A similar view of the economic functions of education is probably roughly applicable to post-primary education, and, for that matter, to schooling everywhere.

Planning Educational Systems, p. 27.

36. Thus it has been claimed that,

   The universal association between education and earnings across industries, sectors and occupational categories in all advanced economies suggests that educated workers are more productive in ways that we have hardly begun to analyze: they are more flexible, adapt themselves easily to changing circumstances, act with initiative in problem-solving situations, are quick to guide others, easily assume supervisory responsibilities, and so forth.

M. Blaug, "An Economic Interpretation of the Private Demand for Education", *Economica* 33 (May, 1966): 181.

37. See Page, "Retraining under the Manpower Development Act", pp. 261-62; Cain and Stromsdorfer, "Retraining in West Virginia", pp. 302 and 313; Somers and Stromsdorfer, "Benefit-Cost Analysis of Manpower Retraining", pp. 178 and 181; Stromsdorfer, "Determinants of Economic Success in Retraining the Unemployed", p. 156.

38. Dropouts comprised 32 per cent of all trainees in the West Virginia programs, and 36 per cent of all trainees in the Massachusetts programs studied by Page. In all MDTA programs, dropouts comprised 41 per cent of total enrollees in the fiscal years 1963-68. See Gibbard and Somers, "Government Retraining in West Virginia", p. 25; Page, "Retraining under the Manpower Development Act", p. 262; *The Manpower Report of the President for 1969*, p. 238.

studies assumed that training did not increase the productivity of dropouts, since this assumption conflicts with other criteria employed by these authors in measuring the allocative benefits from training.[39] We may well be interested in comparing the allocative benefits from training different categories of trainees — such as completors of training courses and dropouts from training courses. But it seems elementary that the bases on which we classify trainees should not affect our criteria of whether there were allocative benefits from training.

The Use of Hourly Earnings in Distinguishing Between the Real and Pecuniary Effects of Training Programs

There are methods of estimating the allocative effects of investment in human capital which have not been used in past analyses of MDTA-type training programs, but which appear to offer the best available solutions to the problems created by pecuniary effects of these programs. Several writers have argued that hourly earnings are superior to annual earnings as an indicator of the productivity of workers, on the grounds that the latter measure of earnings also incorporates the effects of both voluntary and involuntary allocation of time to earning activities.[40] The latter reasons do not entirely constitute conclusive support for the argument that hourly wage rates are the best measure of the productivity of workers; in industries which are subject to seasonal and cyclical fluctuations in output, it is possible that workers are paid higher hourly wage rates to compensate for the irregularity of their employment. There is some doubt as to whether such "compensatory effects" exercise an important effect on hourly earnings, but for the most part, information on these compensatory

39.   Thus Page assumed that training increased the productivity of workers who both completed their courses of instruction and were subsequently employed in the field for which they were trained. However, it is clear that dropouts may also "use" skills acquired in training courses in subsequent employment. Borus also considered that training only increased the real output of society if trainees subsequently obtained jobs using skills acquired in training. But because Borus found dropouts who satisfied this condition, he made no distinction between completors and dropouts in assessing the allocative effects of training programs.

In the studies of West Virginia programs the allocative benefits from training were considered to be the difference between the average earnings levels of graduates of training programs and the average earnings levels of control groups of workers who were not trained, after allowing for the effects on earnings associated with the nontraining characteristics of individuals. But the reasoning which supports the inference that there were allocative benefits from training workers who completed courses of instruction, also supports the inference that there were allocative benefits from training workers who did not complete courses of instruction. Thus the regression analysis undertaken by Stromsdorfer reveals that, net of the effects associated with the nontraining characteristics of individuals, the average earnings levels of dropouts from training courses were higher than the average earnings levels of the control group of workers who never entered training. See "Determinants of Economic Success in Retraining the Unemployed", pp. 145-46.

40.   See for instance Jacob Mincer, "The Distribution of Labor Incomes: A Survey with Special Reference to the Human Capital Approach", *Journal of Economic Literature* 8 (March, 1970): 24; Morgan and David, "Education and Income", p. 423; Morgan and Sirageldin, "Note on the Quality Dimension of Education", pp. 1069-70; Taussig, "Vocational Education in the New York City High Schools", p. 74.

effects is simply unavailable.[41] Subject to the reservation that hourly wage rates may reflect such compensatory effects, however, this measure of earnings will also be regarded as the best indicator of the productivity of workers in the present study.

Several methods have been proposed for using data on the hourly wage rates of workers to construct estimates of the allocative effects of investments in human capital. Perhaps the best-known of these procedures is that adopted by Morgan and David. These writers have estimated the returns to education on the basis of what annual earnings level would be if members of the labor force worked for the same number of hours per year at prevailing hourly wage levels.[42] This method of calculating the allocative effects of education rests on the critical assumption that unemployment can and should be removed by raising aggregate demand in the economy.[43] To take account of this viewpoint, the allocative effects of the training sponsored by MITCE will be calculated by the method suggested by Morgan and David. However, this procedure will not be adopted as the primary method of measuring the allocative effects of training in our study.

Taussig has suggested an alternative method of using data on the hourly wage rates of workers to estimate the allocative effects of training programs which is consistent with both the deficient aggregate demand and "structural" theories of the causation of unemployment. Taussig argues that if training programs are associated with significant increases in both the hourly wage rates and the employment of trainees, then the employment effects associated with the training may be assumed to represent genuine increases in aggregate employment, since the wage rate increases indicate that trainees have entered jobs requiring higher productivity.[44] Thus where training is associated with

---

41. The writer knows of only one empirical study which throws light on the alleged compensatory effect, and this study does not reveal the expected theoretical relationship between the stability of employment in industries and the average hourly wage rates paid to workers. Thus the regression coefficients in Weiss' study indicate that industries in which employment was subject to marked cyclical fluctuations paid significantly *lower* average hourly wage rates to workers than other industries. See Leonard W. Weiss, "Concentration and Labor Earnings", *American Economic Review* 56 (March, 1966): 99 and 109.

42. "Education and Income", p. 433.

43. *Ibid.*, p. 423. Morgan and David also argue that this method of calculating the allocative effects of education avoids the difficulty that more educated workers take some of the benefits of their higher productivity in the form of increased leisure. The findings of other researchers raise doubts about the validity of the latter argument. For instance, Finegan found that the hours of work and education of employed adult males were positively correlated in a study using U.S. Census of Population data for 1940 and 1950. More recently, Schwartzman's study of data from the 1960 U.S. Census of Population also shows that education is associated with increases in the hours of work of employed persons in nonagricultural industries. See T. Aldrich Finegan, "Hours of Work in the United States: A Cross-Sectional Analysis", *Journal of Political Economy* 70 (Oct., 1962): 459; David Schwartzman, "The Contribution of Education to the Quality of Labor, 1929-1963", *American Economic Review* 58 (June, 1968): 512.

44. "Vocational Education in the New York City High Schools", p. 74.

increases in the hourly wage rates of trainees, it follows from Taussig's argument that the entire annual increase in earnings associated with training represents an increase in the output of the economy. Since the stated intention of Congress in enacting the Manpower Development and Training Act was to combat the problem of structural unemployment, it seems entirely appropriate to use Taussig's criteria in estimating the allocative effects of training programs financed under the Act. Accordingly, the procedure suggested by Taussig will be the method adopted in our text to estimate the allocative effects of training undertaken in the MITCE project.

The Real and Pecuniary Effects of Training Programs Studied in Past Benefit-Cost Analyses

It is relevant to enquire how our criteria of whether training leads to increases in the productivity of workers would have affected the conclusions of past benefit-cost analyses of MDTA-type training programs. None of the authors of these past analyses determined whether training was in fact associated with increases in the hourly wage rates of workers. However, several of these authors provide data on both the changes in total earnings and the changes in employment which were associated with training in the survey periods of their analyses. These data allow us to infer whether the training programs studied in past analyses were associated with increases in the hourly wage rates of workers.

No previous analysis demonstrates unambiguously that the increase in the earnings of workers which were found to be associated with training were attributable to increases in the hourly wage rates of trainees. On the contrary, the evidence available in these studies seems to indicate that the increases in earnings associated with training were entirely attributable to increases in the employment of workers. Thus Borus notes specifically that the $500 annual improvement in the incomes of workers who used their training was primarily due to a five week reduction in their expected annual levels of unemployment, and that the hourly wage rates of the workers in his three control groups were " . . . approximately the same" as those of workers who proceeded to use their training.[45] Stromsdorfer's analysis throws the clearest light on the employment and wage effects associated with the various West Virginia training programs. The regression coefficients for training status in Stromsdorfer's study indicate that the net earnings of nontrainees were 30 per cent less than those of training completors in the survey period, due to the fact that nontrainees were employed 31 per cent less of the time.[46] In other words, the entire increase in earnings

45. "Benefit-Cost Analysis of Retraining the Unemployed", pp. 381 and 422. In actual fact, the average hourly wage rates of members of two of the control groups were higher at the end of the survey period than the average hourly wage rate of workers who used their training. *Ibid.*, p. 381.

46. Stromsdorfer suggested in earlier drafts of his published study that the performance of training completors could be compared in relative terms to that of nontrainees by dividing the net regression coefficient for training completors by the intercept term in his regression equations. This suggestion has been used in reaching the conclusions noted in the text. For the data, see Stromsdorfer, "Determinants of Economic Success in Retraining the Unemployed", p. 150.

associated with the West Virginia training programs was attributable to increases in the employment of trainees. Page provides less information on the point in question than other authors. Nevertheless, Page does indicate that the increases in earnings associated with the Massachusetts training programs he studied were accompanied by a substantial decline in welfare and unemployment compensation payments to trainees.[47] It is therefore a fair deduction that the increases in earnings associated with these Massachusetts training programs were also attributable in large part to improvement in the employment records of trainees. Finally, it is relevant to note that a study restricted to analysis of the *benefits* from MDTA training also concludes that " . . . the MDTA program does increase employment, even if it does not lead to better paying jobs".[48]

The fact that the training programs studied in past analyses were not apparently associated with any increases in the hourly wage rates of workers raises the obvious possibility that the employment effects associated with these programs did not represent allocative benefits to society, but were simply transfers of income from nonparticipants in training programs to trainees. The latter possibility cannot be lightly dismissed, in view of the special efforts that were made to find jobs for completors of these training programs and the slack labor markets prevailing in the survey periods of analyses of these programs. It is of course possible that the trainees in these programs were paid somewhat lower hourly wage rates to compensate for the fact that their employment was more stable than that of nontrainees. In these circumstances, training might raise the productivity of workers without raising their hourly wage rates. However, there is additional evidence which supports the view that the job-placement activities of training program officials played a substantial part in bringing about the increases in employment associated with completing these training programs. The evidence comes principally from the studies of West Virginia training programs, where earnings and employment data were collected for somewhat longer periods than in other benefit-cost analyses, and where trainees and nontrainees were also subsequently reinterviewed four to five years after training was completed. Both the original interviews and the reinterviews of sample members in the West Virginia studies indicate that " . . . the [employment] advantages gained by retraining may begin to wash out after years of general employment expansion".[49] A similar decline over time in employment

---

47. "Retraining under the Manpower Development Act", p. 262.

48. Main, "A Nationwide Evaluation of MDTA Job Training", p. 159.

49. Gerald G. Somers and Graeme H. McKechnie, "Vocational Retraining Programs for the Unemployed", *Proceedings of the Twentieth Annual Winter Meeting, Industrial Relations Research Association* (Madison, Wis., 1967), p. 34. See also Cain and Stromsdorfer, "Retraining in West Virginia", p. 322; Gibbard and Somers, "Government Retraining in West Virginia", p. 88. It should be noted that Borus also undertook a follow-up study of respondents in his original survey of trainees and nontrainees in Connecticut. The follow-up study provided earnings and employment data for a period of five years after the completion of training programs, and led Borus to conclude that the benefits from training grew over this time interval. The writer is not inclined to accept Borus' conclusion, in view

differentials between completors of training programs and nontrainees has also been observed by Solie in his analysis of the increases in employment associated with MDTA-type training programs in Tennessee.[50] Such declines in the employment effects associated with completing training programs are, of course, precisely to be expected where these employment differentials are attributable to the job-placement activities of training program officials.[51]

If the training programs studied in past benefit-cost analyses led to no allocative benefits, and simply transferred income to trainees from nonparticipants in training programs, there are several important implications for policy in the antipoverty program as a whole. In the first place, training courses would appear to be an expensive method of achieving transfer payments, in terms of the allocative costs incurred in the operation of these courses. Secondly, any such transfer payments occurring as a result of training programs are surely not the kind of income redistribution which the antipoverty program is intended to bring about. The pecuniary effects of training programs are, at best, transfers of income between individuals in similar economic circumstances. However, it is also possible that such transfer payments could be regressive in their impact on the distribution of incomes. We noted earlier that the trainees in programs studied in past analyses were selected from among the unemployed on the basis of their performance on aptitude and intelligence tests. Individuals who passed these tests were therefore more likely to improve their economic status than those who did not. Thus, if the training programs studied in past analyses simply led to trainees obtaining jobs which would otherwise have gone to unemployed members of the labor force, it appears that individuals who were on average more fortunate were being helped at the expense of those who were less fortunate.

Our examination of the effects of training on the productivity of workers studied in past benefit-cost analyses of MDTA-type training has therefore led to pessimistic conclusions in terms of the objectives of the antipoverty program. It remains to be seen whether our analysis of the training undertaken in the MITCE project will show training programs to be more successful as an antipoverty measure.

Psychic, Consumption, and External Benefits from Training Programs

To this point, our analysis of the real benefits from training has been concerned with the problems of identifying and valuing any increases in output

---

of the fact that when no distinctions were made among nontrainees according to their reasons for not taking training, the result was that training was not associated with increases in earnings at the .05 significance level. See Michael E. Borus, "Time Trends in the Benefits from Retraining in Connecticut", *Proceedings of the Twentieth Annual Winter Meeting, Industrial Relations Research Association* (Madison, Wis., 1967), pp. 41-43.

50. "Employment Effects of Retraining the Unemployed", p. 222.

51. As at least two other benefit-cost analysts have observed. See Cain and Stromsdorfer, "Retraining in West Virginia", pp. 322-23.

which may be associated with training programs. But training may well give rise to other real benefits, including nonmonetary benefits to trainees and indirect benefits to "third parties" not participating in training programs. No attempt will be made in the present study to measure these additional real effects of training programs. However, for reasons which will be outlined below, it is debatable whether these omissions will significantly affect our evaluation of the MITCE project.

Those who have viewed the process of schooling as investment in human capital have frequently been accused of ignoring "psychic" and consumption benefits from schooling. For instance, education may increase the satisfaction an individual derives from the use of his leisure time, or enable him to obtain jobs where nonmonetary satisfactions are greater. To the extent that such psychic income streams accrue to the individual after the completion of his education, they are just as much returns on an investment as any monetary income streams deriving from education. In addition, the real costs of education to the individual may be reduced if he obtains psychic or consumption benefits during the process of schooling. To the extent that nonmonetary benefits of any of these kinds are ignored, the returns from education will, of course, be underestimated.

There are marked differences of opinion as to the importance of the psychic or consumption benefits from schooling.[52] Such differences of opinion are understandable, since there have been few concrete suggestions as to how some of these benefits can be measured. One would expect, however, that the failure to measure these nonmonetary income streams would be less serious in the context of the present study. For instance, the arguments that schooling may be accompanied by current consumption benefits or lead to future satisfactions from the use of leisure time would seem more germane to an evaluation of a liberal arts education than to an evaluation of antipoverty training programs.

Many of the postulated externalities of schooling also seem more likely to be associated with general education or higher education than with antipoverty training programs.[53] However, there are at least two widely-advertised ways in which training programs are expected to benefit parties not participating in the programs. One of the objectives of the Manpower Development and Training Act is " ... to reduce the costs of unemployment compensation and public assistance".[54] It is also frequently claimed that training programs may reduce

---

52. For a critical analysis of the argument that there are positive psychic benefits from education, see M. Blaug, "The Rate of Return on Investment in Education", *The Manchester Journal* 33 (Sept., 1965): 218-19.

53. For comprehensive catalogues of the possible external benefits of education, see Blaug, "The Rate of Return on Investment in Education", pp. 234-35, and Burton A. Weisbrod, *External Benefits of Public Education: An Economic Analysis* (Princeton, N.J.: Princeton University, Department of Economics, Industrial Relations Section, 1964).

54. See Section 101 of the Manpower Development and Training Act.

juvenile delinquency and other forms of antisocial behavior. It is possible to obtain some notion of the magnitude of the real benefits from such side-effects of training programs.

It is worth stressing that training programs may have no effects on the levels of transfer payments or antisocial behavior unless these programs also lead to net increases in national income. If training programs merely transfer jobs and income from nontrainees to trainees, obviously there may be no overall reduction in the levels of unemployment compensation or welfare payments. Juvenile delinquency and antisocial behavior may also be negatively related to the income of individuals and positively related to their unemployment rates.[55] Again, if training programs merely shift the burden of low incomes and unemployment from trainees to nontrainees, there may also be no net reduction in the level of antisocial behavior.

In addition, care must be taken to distinguish the "real" costs from the "pecuniary" effects of transfer payments and antisocial behavior. For instance, the real costs of direct income redistribution include the opportunity costs of the resources involved in the distribution and financing of transfer payments, and any loss in output attributable to disincentives to work for those receiving the transfer payments or for those taxed to provide the transfer payments. Similarly, the real costs of antisocial behavior include the costs of harm to persons and damage to property, the costs of resources involved in law enforcement, and the disincentive effects on output of the taxation necessary to finance law enforcement.

The corresponding real benefits from any reduction in the level of antisocial behavior are likely to be small in relation to any increases in the productivity of workers which are associated with training programs. According to Fleisher, " . . . a 10 per cent rise in income may be expected to reduce delinquency rates by between 15 and 20 per cent when the income change occurs in highly delinquent areas and is of the type that will reduce the number of broken families as well".[56] Ribich has in turn used this finding to make rough estimates of the savings in expenditures on law enforcement which are likely to result from income growth in high-delinquency areas. It appears that the potential cost savings are approximately one-half of one per cent of any increase in average family incomes, and Ribich does not think the order of magnitude of such savings would be substantially altered by finer calculations.[57]

---

55. The relationships between income, unemployment and delinquency noted in the text are those found by Fleisher. However, Fleisher's conclusions have recently been questioned and the issues raised in criticism of his work are far from being resolved. See Belton M. Fleisher, "The Effect of Income on Delinquency", *American Economic Review* 56 (March, 1966): 118-37; John C. Weicher, "Comment", and Belton M. Fleisher, "Reply", *ibid.* 60 (March, 1970): 249-56 and 257.

56. "The Effect of Income on Delinquency", p. 135.

57. *Education and Poverty,* p. 121.

Theoretical and Empirical Problems

Unfortunately, similar estimates of the real benefits arising from reductions in transfer payments are unavailable at the present time.[58] Yet it is reasonable to suppose that the real benefits from this possible side-effect of training programs are also likely to be low. In this connection, it is perhaps significant that many benefit-cost analysts are prepared to ignore the distributional consequences of public expenditure programs, on the grounds that any unfavorable distributional outcomes can be remedied without significant allocative costs to society by means of direct redistribution of income.[59] In conclusion, therefore, it appears that little will be lost by ignoring the external benefits which are claimed to result from training programs.[60]

THE ALLOCATIVE COSTS OF TRAINING

We propose to measure the real benefits from the MITCE project by valuing the increases in output that are associated with training. Similarly, in measuring the real costs of training, we need to estimate the value of the resources which were lost to society because the MITCE project was undertaken.[61] The principles which will be followed in estimating these allocative costs of training are those outlined in Becker's models of schooling and on-the-job training. However, we need to indicate how these models should be amended to take account of the fact that most of the costs of MDTA training are borne by the public purse. Since slightly different problems are encountered in measuring the allocative costs of institutional and on-the-job training, these topics will now be considered separately in our analysis.

Government expenditures incurred in connection with MDTA institutional training courses comprise both capital and noncapital items. Most of the current expenses associated with the operation of these training courses — such as the

---

58. The most difficult problem in calculating the allocative costs of direct income redistribution would appear to be in estimating the effects on the supply of labor. A summary of research on this subject suggests that " . . . evidence on the probable effects of representative transfer-by-taxation plans on work incentives is inconclusive". Christopher Green, *Negative Taxes and the Poverty Problem* (Washington, D.C.: The Brookings Institution, 1967), p. 12.

59. See, for instance, the views noted by Samuel B. Chase, Jr., "Introduction", and Burton A. Weisbrod, "Income Redistribution Effects and Benefit-Cost Analysis", in *Problems in Public Expenditure Analysis,* ed. Samuel B. Chase, Jr. (Washington, D.C.: The Brookings Institution, 1968), pp. 20-25 and 182-83.

60. This conclusion can hardly be described as novel, in view of findings from analyses of the side-effects from other antipoverty programs. For instance, one would expect that nonvocational schooling might give rise to greater psychic and consumption benefits for the individual, and greater benefits for third parties, than would vocational training. Yet in a careful and comprehensive survey, Ribich concludes that an evaluation of such side-effects " . . . does not add a great deal to 'the case for education' as it applies to the goal of poverty reduction". See *Education and Poverty,* p. 124.

61. Our treatment of the real costs of training will be symmetrical with our treatment of the real benefits from training in that we will not attempt to measure possible psychic costs to trainees or indirect costs to third parties not participating in training programs.

salaries of instructors or of personnel providing supporting services for training, and the costs of raw materials used in training – can be included directly in our estimates of the allocative costs of training. However, the transfer payments provided for the support of participants in these training courses do not represent opportunity costs for society. The administrative costs incurred in the disbursement of these trainee allowances will be included in our estimates of the allocative costs of training. As we have seen, estimates of other possible allocative costs of transfer payments are as yet unavailable.

The treatment of capital costs incurred for institutional training courses presents greater problems for our analysis. The official cost data for institutional training courses in which MITCE clients participated include the costs of purchases of equipment and alterations of plant, but do not reflect the costs of the use of public facilities which were already in existence when the courses were undertaken. Moreover, the equipment purchased for the courses in which MITCE clients participated was subsequently used in other MDTA courses and even in activities not connected with MDTA training. In principle, the solution to these problems is to impute a rental value for the use of plant and equipment by MITCE trainees. In practice, it will be seen that there are considerable difficulties in obtaining the appropriate opportunity cost data for the use of plant and equipment in these institutional training courses, and more rough-and-ready allowances will need to be made for these costs.

Becker's analysis of the allocative cost of schooling emphasizes the importance of output forgone because students are in the classroom when they could be working. Following Becker's model, estimates of what institutional trainees could have earned had they not been in training will be used to represent the costs of such forgone output for society. Allowances for the forgone earnings of trainees can make an appreciable difference to assessments of the allocative effects of institutional training courses. With the exception of the studies of West Virginia training programs, past benefit-cost analyses have not included such estimates of the forgone earnings of trainees in their calculations of the allocative costs of MDTA-type training programs. However, Cain and Stromsdorfer indicate that forgone earnings constituted 26 per cent of the allocative costs of training women and 45 per cent of the allocative costs of training men in the West Virginia programs they studied.[62] These estimates of the relative importance of forgone earnings in the allocative costs of institutional training for men are comparable to findings from studies of the allocative costs of education.[63]

---

62. In calculating the proportion of allocative costs of these programs which were made up of forgone earnings, transfer payments were excluded from the cost data provided by Cain and Stromsdorfer. For the data, see "Retraining in West Virginia", p. 313.

63. For instance, Schultz has estimated that forgone earnings constituted 43 per cent of the allocative costs of United States primary, secondary and college education in 1956. Forgone earnings made up the somewhat higher proportion of three-fifths of the allocative costs of high school and college education considered alone. See Theodore W. Schultz, "Capital Formation by Education", *Journal of Political Economy* 68 (Dec., 1960): 577 and 582.

Substantial public expenditures were also incurred in providing on-the-job training for MITCE clients. Our estimate is that the allocative costs of recruiting MITCE clients for on-the-job training, of arranging on-the-job training contracts with employers, and of providing counselling services for on-the-job trainees, amounted to roughly $1,200 per MITCE client. In addition, subsidies of $68 per female MITCE client and $108 per male MITCE client were paid directly to employers who undertook on-the-job training contracts. However, the treatment of these subsidies requires a closer examination in our analysis of the allocative costs of training.

In Becker's models of general and specific on-the-job training, the opportunity costs of training which are not borne by firms are the wages forgone by trainees during the period of instruction.[64] No such costs, in fact, appear to have been incurred by the average MITCE on-the-job trainee. Employers sponsoring on-the-job training for MITCE clients were required to comply with legal minimum-wage provisions during the training period, and the regression analysis in our study will indicate that the "expected" wages trainees would have received had they not been in training were lower than those they actually received in the training period. It therefore appears that the government subsidy to employers undertaking on-the-job training of MITCE clients was partly a reimbursement for administering a transfer payment. Of course, the disbursement of such transfer payments would involve the use of resources which have opportunity costs — irrespective of who distributes these payments. However, in view of the comparatively minor sums involved, it was not felt worthwhile to make more detailed enquiries as to what proportion of these subsidies to employers represented "real" costs, and what proportion represented transfer payments to trainees. Our treatment of these subsidies to employers as being allocative costs of training will accordingly represent an overestimate of the resources that were forgone by society because MITCE clients were trained.

INTEGRATION OF DISTRIBUTIONAL AND ALLOCATIVE CRITERIA IN AN EVALUATION OF MITCE

Our evaluation of MITCE will consist in establishing what difference the project made to the incomes of the poor, and what effect the project had on the allocation of resources within the economy. These separate indicators of the effects of the project will need to be integrated in order to reach an overall judgment on the success of MITCE. In some cases, integration of our distributional and allocative criteria will allow us to reach firm conclusions as to whether MITCE was a success or a failure. In other cases, the criteria may

---

64. It will be recalled that the data from our survey of MITCE clients do not permit us to estimate any of the returns from "specific" on-the-job training which accrue to firms. Accordingly, consistency requires that our estimates of the allocative costs of on-the-job training should also exclude any of the costs of specific training which are incurred by firms.

conflict and we cannot determine whether a project with such distributional and allocative effects should be regarded as successful or not. Nevertheless, it will be seen that even where the criteria conflict, our analysis may serve a useful purpose in policy formulation merely by presenting the available data on the distributional and allocative outcomes of the MITCE project.

The one basic criterion which must, of course, be satisfied by any antipoverty project is that the incomes of the poor should be raised. Administrators of an antipoverty program would allocate no more funds to projects where this condition was not fulfilled. It is equally obvious that any antipoverty project which satisfies this criterion and has an allocative benefit-cost ratio at least equal to unity will represent a desirable method to society of reducing poverty. Such an outcome implies that while resources have been diverted from alternative uses in order to reduce poverty, there have been no real costs to society in the process. In other words, society has not had to reduce output in order to raise the incomes of the poor.

Apart from instances where projects involve no net allocative costs to society and also redistribute income to the poor, few clear policy prescriptions are possible in an analysis of the distributive and allocative effects of antipoverty programs. In particular it will *not* be assumed in the present analysis that any antipoverty program which is allocatively inefficient is also undesirable as a distributional measure. The latter position has occasionally been adopted in analyses of antipoverty programs.[65]

The position that no antipoverty measure should be undertaken if its allocative benefit-cost ratio is estimated to be less than unity arises from analogies to the costs of income redistribution by means of taxation and transfer payments. Proponents of this viewpoint often take the position that the allocative costs of direct income redistribution are so small that they can afford to be ignored by society. Equally, of course, there are those who maintain that the costs of such direct income redistribution may not be insignificant.[66] Needless to say, differences of opinion on this issue can only arise because satisfactory estimates of the allocative costs of direct income redistribution are not yet available. Thus at present we cannot specify, for each dollar by which the income of the poor is raised, any level of costs at which we would be indifferent *on allocative grounds* between the use of transfer payments and other antipoverty measures. By the same token, until the allocative costs of direct income redistribution are known, we cannot assume that any antipoverty measure which is allocatively inefficient is also "inefficient" as a distributional measure.

65. See for instance Glen G. Cain, *Benefit-Cost Estimates for Job Corps* (Madison, Wis.: Institute for Research on Poverty, The University of Wisconsin, 1967), p. 2, and Glen G. Cain and Robinson W. Hollister, "Evaluating Manpower Programs for the Disadvantaged", in *Cost-Benefit Analysis of Manpower Policies,* p. 124.

66. See the sources cited in footnote 59 above.

However, there is a good reason why we should not regard the allocative costs of transfer payments as dictating an upper limit to the costs society would be prepared to incur in undertaking other antipoverty measures. Among both policymakers and the public at large, there appears to be an aversion to the use of transfer payments in reducing poverty, and a linked belief that the poor should be made better off by working. The official goal of the antipoverty program — "to change people from 'poor' to 'nonpoor' *through their own efforts*" — reflects these beliefs. It follows that even if transfer payments were completely costless in allocative terms, society might still be prepared to undertake alternative antipoverty measures which were allocatively inefficient.

Of course, this preference among antipoverty instruments needs to be interpreted with caution as a guide to the costs which would be acceptable in antipoverty measures other than transfer payments. A preference for reducing poverty by increasing the earnings levels of the poor does not imply that such measures will *always* be preferred to transfer payments. Direct income redistribution must be an element in any comprehensive attack on poverty, if only because some of the poor — whether because of old age, or physical or mental infirmities — cannot be expected to obtain higher incomes by working. Moreover, even where it is feasible to reduce poverty by measures which increase the earnings levels of the poor, it is unlikely that these measures would be preferred to transfer payments under all circumstances. Presumably, policymakers in an antipoverty program will have an implicit trade-off function between the goal of reducing poverty in itself and the goal of reducing poverty by means of raising the earnings levels of the poor. Of course, accurate estimates of the allocative costs of transfer payments are a prerequisite for the construction of an explicit trade-off function between these goals. But benefit-cost analyses of antipoverty measures other than transfer payments can also help make such a trade-off function explicit, by providing information on the real costs to society of allocatively inefficient antipoverty measures. Thus even where it is not possible to determine whether projects are successful antipoverty measures, presentation of data on the distributional and allocative effects of these projects may serve as a useful aid to policy formulation in an antipoverty program.

CHAPTER III

THE BENEFITS FROM TRAINING IN THE SURVEY PERIOD

In order to estimate the distributional and allocative benefits from the training undertaken by MITCE, it is first necessary to find the change in earnings associated with training in the period covered by our survey of MITCE clients. Other objectives in our analysis of data from the survey of MITCE clients are to establish whether the type of instruction received by trainees (i.e. on-the-job or institutional training), the sex of the trainee, the occupations for which training took place, and whether training was completed or not, were associated with significant differences in the earnings of MITCE clients. Considerable interest is also attached to determining whether training served to offset characteristics of MITCE clients considered to convey disadvantages in the labor market. Regression analysis of the data from our survey of MITCE clients will be employed to attain the objectives we have listed.

The principal dependent variable in our regression analysis will be the average weekly earnings of MITCE clients in the after-training period. Trainees were interviewed, on average, 68.9 weeks after they completed their training (the standard deviation being 17.3 weeks). This information was used to construct a fictional "after-training" period for the nontrainees who comprise the control group in our analysis; their earnings were aggregated for the period beginning after the mean quarter in which trainees completed their courses of instruction. The earnings of MITCE clients in the after-training period were averaged on a weekly basis to control for differences in the lengths of time for which data were available for individual survey respondents.

Two additional dependent variables which will be used in our regression analysis were created by disaggregating average weekly earnings in the after-training period to obtain the average hourly earnings of respondents and the average number of hours they worked per week. We need to establish whether any changes in hourly earnings were associated with the training of MITCE clients, in order to infer whether there were any allocative benefits from training. The changes associated with training in the amount of work obtained by MITCE clients are of closely related interest in our analysis.

THE TYPE OF REGRESSION ANALYSIS EMPLOYED IN THE STUDY

The form of regression analysis used in our study was influenced by some of the features of the data collected in the survey of MITCE clients. The problems encountered here were common to other cross-section studies where a wealth of data has been collected on the characteristics of individual respondents.

The first of these problems is that the effects of a characteristic on the dependent variable may not be linear and the use of linear regression techniques will yield "biased" estimates.[1] An example of nonlinearity which is often cited is the effect of age on labor force participation rates, employment and incomes: when the effects of other socio-economic variables are held constant, both younger and older workers are thought to have difficulty in finding employment as compared to those in the "prime" age groups.

Where the presence of nonlinearity is suspected, the use of "dummy" rather than continuous variables will yield unbiased coefficients, providing the dummy categories chosen are not grossly inaccurate. Of course, irrespective of the presence of nonlinearity, the use of dummy variables is called for where a characteristic cannot be conventionally scaled. Examples of such variables in our analysis are the MITCE target area in which the respondent lived, his race, sex and the occupation for which he was trained. The fact that many of the characteristics used in the analysis had to be represented as dummy variables, together with the suspected presence of nonlinearity in much of the remainder, led to the decision to use dummy variables exclusively, for the sake of uniformity.

The fact remains, however, that in multiple regression analysis the coefficients are treated as if they were additive, and this interpretation is spurious where interaction effects occur. The detection of interaction effects is a second major problem in cross-section studies. An example of such an interaction effect would be the effect on a respondent's earnings of the number of years of education he received and the quality of education he obtained. Where interaction effects were suspected among the independent variables used in our analysis, our main attack was to develop "combination" variables which synthesized information on the characteristics concerned. For instance, data on the respondent's final grade level and the quality of his education were combined to form a single composite variable.

Another commonly employed method of dealing with interaction effects is to run separate regressions for affected subgroups of the population. This strategy was not adopted specifically in our study, but its objectives may have been achieved indirectly in some cases. An aim of our analysis was to discover whether training was associated with net increases in the earnings of "disadvantaged" groups in the population. Thus, separate consecutive regressions

---

1.   The term "biased" is used in this sense by Daniel B. Suits, "The Use of Dummy Variables in Regression Equations", *Journal of the American Statistical Association* 52 (Dec., 1967): 551.

were run to find the net changes in earnings associated with training for the following subgroups: nonwhites, women, older workers, youths, respondents who had little education or who had farmed or been unemployed for long intervals in the pre-training period. To the extent that there were interactions between training status and these characteristics of disadvantage in the labor market, the problem would be eliminated in these separate regressions.[2]

The Independent Variables Used in the Regressions

There were several main objectives in the selection of independent variables for use in the regressions. It was hoped to capture not only the more obvious physical and motivational characteristics of the respondents, but also their different embodiments of human capital. It was also considered desirable to measure the effects of wider environmental influences which might affect the earnings and employment experience of respondents.

Respondents were first classified according to the *target area* in which they were recruited for training. MITCE's operations were confined to three such areas: Craven County; Nash and Edgecombe Counties; and Richmond, Robeson and Scotland Counties. With a handful of exceptions, respondents were also employed and interviewed in the same target area in which they were recruited for training. The agricultural and industrial structure of the economies of the three target areas varies considerably; therefore, this variable will take into account differences in the amount and type of work available to respondents in each location.

Past *mobility* of respondents was measured in terms of the number of states in which they had lived since joining the labor force. Migration is one means whereby an individual obtains information about his social and economic environment: it is part of the continuing process of education.[3] Our presumption was that a respondent who had seen wider horizons would be better equipped for the local job market than one who had never been outside, say, Craven County. As Morgan and his colleagues note, the mobility of a respondent may also be a proxy for ambition, with nonlinear effects: "Very little movement may mean lack of ambition, while a great deal may indicate instability or irresponsibility."[4]

A *veteran status* variable was included on the basis of much the same kind of reasoning as the mobility variable. It was expected that military service would sharpen the individual's perception of job opportunities. Veterans may also have acquired job skills in service which serve them in good stead in civilian life. There

---

2. For an account of the issues raised by interaction effects in cross-section studies, see James N. Morgan and John A. Sonquist, "Problems in the Analysis of Survey Data and a Proposal", *Journal of the American Statistical Association* 58 (June, 1963): 415-34.

3. I am indebted to Charles Fairchild for first making this point to me.

4. James N. Morgan, *et al., Income and Welfare in the United States* (New York: McGraw-Hill, 1962), p. 47.

is also the possibility, of course, that employers may discriminate in favour of veterans where job applicants who are equally qualified present themselves.

A *"prior labor force experience"* variable was included in the analysis on the grounds that this factor would considerably affect earnings after training. The problem was to construct an independent variable that would yield this information and yet be something more than a reflection of the dependent variables used in the analysis. Eventually, a variable formulated by Stromsdorfer was adapted to serve this purpose.[5] The status of the respondent when he was first contacted by MITCE was initially classified as follows: not in the labor force, farm worker, nonfarm worker, or unemployed. Unemployed respondents were further differentiated according to whether they had been continuously without work for periods of less than 6 months or periods of 6 months or more before they were recruited for training. This distinction was made in an effort to differentiate previous unemployment according to whether it was transitory or long-term in nature. The hypothesis underlying the use of the prior labor force experience variable was that the respondent who had a background of regular nonfarm employment before training would be more likely to have higher net earnings after training than other sample members.

As noted above, it was expected that the *age* predictor would exert a nonlinear influence on earnings. This is, of course, the reason why the MDTA Guidelines specify that youths and older workers should be given preference in admission to training programs.

The *physical condition* of the respondent would be measured indirectly in the age variable, and was also measured separately in a classification drawn from questionnaire evidence. The respondent was classified according to whether his health or physical handicaps would restrict his work capabilities and appeal to employers in any way, and if so whether moderately or severely.

The *race* and *sex* variables were expected to reveal the familiar pattern of labor market discrimination against women and nonwhites. An interaction effect could operate between these variables, since male and female labor force participation rates differ considerably according to the race of the individual in North Carolina.[6] The idea of forming a combination category of the race and sex variables was discarded, however, in order to allow the sex variable to be used in forming a combination variable dealing with more obvious interaction effects. Specifically, it was considered desirable to produce a *family status* variable which combined information on the sex and family responsibilities of respondents.[7] It was thought that this variable would have a powerful explanatory

---

5. See "Determinants of Economic Success in Retraining the Unemployed", p. 143.

6. See my paper, *Some Implications of Employment Trends in North Carolina, 1950-60* (Durham, N.C.: The North Carolina Fund, 1966), pp. 4-6.

7. Alleged marital status was discarded as a variable in the analysis, on the grounds that it bore little relation to actual family responsibilities.

effect on labor force participation, employment and earnings. For instance, women with young children in the house may have limited job opportunities because of the hours they can work and the distance they can travel. This is especially true where no relatives are available to mind the children, since day nurseries are practically nonexistent in the rural sections of the counties studied.[8] It was also expected that the labor market performance of young males with no family attachments would differ radically from that of other males in the sample.

The outcome of the deliberations over the family status variable was the choice of a set with six elements: males having no dependents, males having dependents not including children under 14 years of age, males having dependents including children, and the same categories for females.

It is customarily expected that, *ceteris paribus,* the more *education* a person has, the higher his earnings level will be. However, as was noted in Chapter I, it was found in testing MITCE clients that the functional level of their education often bore little relation to the amount of education they claimed they had received. With this reservation in mind as to effect, years of education completed by the respondent were entered as an independent variable in the analysis.

Most enquiries into the rates of return to education have made the same simplistic assumption implicit in the construction of our first education variable: i.e., that units of education are homogenous. In recent years, however, several investigators have focused on the rates of return to units of education of differing qualities.[9] This idea was incorporated in the construction of our second education variable. The specific hypothesis tested was that a rural grade school education was inferior to an urban grade school education.[10] Information as to the type of grade school the respondent attended was combined with broad groupings of the quantity of education he received to form a new independent variable.

Some asymmetry exists in interpretation of this variable where the individual's education extended beyond grade school, as in the case of exactly 50 per cent of our respondents. Our assertion was, however, that the quality of grade school education was fundamental to further educational progress. In any

8.   See the *MITCE Final Report,* p. 43.

9.   See for instance Shane J. Hunt, "Income Determinants for College Graduates and the Return to Educational Investment", *Yale Economic Essays* 3 (Fall, 1963): 304-57; Finis Welch, "Measurement of the Quality of Schooling", *American Economic Review* 56 (May, 1966): 379-92; Samuel Bowles, "Towards an Educational Production Function", in *Education, Income and Human Capital,* ed. W. Lee Hansen (New York: National Bureau of Economic Research, 1970), pp. 11-61.

10.   One might well expect this after examining the difference in the value of inputs into rural and urban education. See Welch, "Measurement of the Quality of Schooling", pp. 387-88 and footnotes on these pages.

case, if the respondent did proceed to further education beyond grade school, it was likely, in the counties studied, to be in the same rural or urban setting.

The fact that an individual was educated in a rural school could of course be a proxy for other postulated disadvantages inherent in rural life, such as a restrictive social environment. As a matter of fact, a number of other variables were formulated in an attempt to measure early home and environmental influences which might affect the respondent's subsequent career. Mother's and father's education and father's occupation would convey much information concerning the motivation and market information passed on to children, and these variables have been found to be important in other analyses of education and income levels.[11] Unfortunately, they had to be discarded in our study because of severe problems of item nonresponse. However, most respondents did provide information on the *number of siblings* they had, and we can take this indirect measure of family size as an indicator of the resources which were available to feed, clothe, educate and generally care properly for the children in the respondent's family.

A need which in the writer's opinion is unsatisfied by past benefit-cost analyses of training schemes is an answer to the question of whether trainees had such innate qualities of intelligence or motivation that they would have improved their economic status irrespective of whether they were trained or not. To some extent, of course, variables like the level of education and prior labor force experience of the respondent do reflect these attributes. But many other influences also affect these variables and direct measures of "drive" are infinitely preferable.

Morgan and his colleagues have pioneered in the construction of tests of *motivation* which can be used in surveys such as ours and which have sound theoretical and empirical backing. These tests were adapted for use in our questionnaire, and are more fully described in Appendix C.

Finally, the objectives of our analysis required that the *training status* of the respondent be classified in different levels of detail. Three different training status variables were accordingly developed. In the first training status set, the respondent was simply classified according to whether he was a trainee or non-trainee. The second training status set distinguished between the types of instruction received by MITCE trainees; the respondent being classified as an on-the-job trainee, institutional trainee, or a nontrainee. In the third training status set, MITCE trainees were further classified according to whether they completed or failed to complete their training. The five training status categories in this set were on-the-job training completors and dropouts, institutional training completors and dropouts, and nontrainees.

---

11. See for instance Harvey E. Brazer and Martin David, "Social and Economic Determinants of the Demand for Education", in U.S., Department of Health, Education and Welfare, Office of Education, *Economics of Higher Education,* ed. Selma J. Mushkin, (Washington, D.C.: Government Printing Office, 1962), pp. 21-42.

Choosing the Independent Variables

A large number of variables which could possibly have an influence on the earnings and employment levels of MITCE clients have been presented. In order to reduce the regression equations to manageable size, it was necessary to make a choice among the independent variables listed above. It was decided to retain in the regression equations only those sets of characteristics which contained at least one significant element. This procedure eliminated the veteran status set, the number of siblings set, and all but one of the need-achievement sets. However, this cut-off mechanism did not resolve the issue as to whether the family status variable should be preferred to its subset, the sex of the respondent; nor did it determine which of the two education variables was superior. In these cases, the competing regression equations were inspected to see which had the highest coefficient of determination adjusted for degrees of freedom. The family status set and the quantity of education set were preferred to their rivals on the basis of this criterion.

Interpreting the Regression Results

The first fruits of our regression analysis are presented in Table 5. An explanation of the mode of presentation of the data in Table 5 will serve as an introduction to interpretation of the data in this table and other tables to follow.

While the number of respondents for whom data was collected is indicated in Table 5, it should be noted that *all* of the regressions carried out in the present study were weighted regressions. The weights attached to an interview were the reciprocal of the product of the sampling rate and the response rate for the sample category in which the interview occurred. Further details concerning sample and response rates by sample category are given in Appendix A.

The particular dummy variable technique used in regressions in this study was that of partitioning the independent variables into "sets" of mutually exclusive categories, assigning the value of one to the class of which the respondent was a member and zero to the other categories. In regressions using this technique, one element of each set has to be dropped to avoid overdetermination where a constant term is present in the equation. The dropped elements in the several sets are indicated by zeros in the tables incorporating regression results.[12] The other partial regression coefficients attached to the subclasses of a set then indicate the effect on the dependent variable of membership in that class as compared to membership in the dropped class, net of the effect of other independent variables.[13] Thus Table 5 shows, for

---

12. The category dropped from each set in most cases represented the modal characteristic of respondents.

13. For further explanation of this technique and examples of its use, see Morgan *et al., Income and Welfare in the United States,* Appendix E, and Stromsdorfer, "Determinants of Economic Success in Retraining the Unemployed", *passim.*

The Benefits From Training

Table 5: Multiple Regression of Weekly Earnings after Training, and the Components of Weekly Earnings after Training, on Respondent Characteristics:

Complete Classification of Training Status[1]

	Earnings per week (dollars)	Hours worked per week	Hourly earnings (cents)
Net regression coefficients:			
Area			
Craven County	- 8.7**	- 4.3**	-12.2**
Nash and Edgecombe Cos.	- 7.8**	- 3.8**	- 9.4**
Richmond, Robeson and Scotland Cos.[2]	0	0	0
Labor force experience prior to training			
Farmer	-11.2**	- 0.3	-33.7**
Held nonfarm job[2]	0	0	0
Unemployed under 6 months	- 5.4**	- 5.6**	- 6.0
Unemployed 6 months or more	-10.0**	-10.5**	6.0
Not in labor force	-12.9**	-13.0**	- 9.1*
Physical limitation			
Moderately handicapped	3.6	0.7	9.7*
Severely handicapped	-20.6**	-14.3**	-34.0**
Not handicapped[2]	0	0	0
Color			
White	14.5**	2.7	15.3*
Nonwhite[2]	0	0	0
Age as of 1 Jan., 1966			
54 years and over	-15.6**	- 9.1**	-27.2**
44 - 53 years	- 8.1**	- 0.6	-18.0**
34 - 43 years	1.9	0.3	- 5.3
21 - 33 years[2]	0	0	0
Under 21 years	2.0	0.4	10.0*
States lived in			
One[2]	0	0	0
More than one	3.5*	- 2.4*	19.5**
Education			
0 - 5 grades[2]	0	0	0
6 - 8 grades	3.2	0.7	- 4.6
9 - 11 grades	5.5**	1.2	4.4
12 grades and over	14.0**	4.6**	18.5**
Need-achievement score			
Lowest third of scores	- 3.0*	0.4	- 2.5
Medium third of scores[2]	0	0	0
Highest third of scores	- 1.3	0.1	- 6.0

Table 5: Continued

	Earnings per week (dollars)	Hours worked per week	Hourly earnings (cents)
Net regression coefficients:			
Family status			
Males, no dependents[2]	0	0	0
Males, dependents not including children	14.7**	6.1**	26.4**
Males, dependents including children	15.8**	7.5**	25.6**
Females, no dependents	-12.1**	- 5.2**	-15.0*
Females, dependents not including children	- 1.5	2.9	0.1
Females, dependents including children	- 9.4**	- 7.3**	- 5.6
Training status			
Nontrainees[2]	0	0	0
On-the-job training completors	11.6**	2.5**	25.4**
On-the-job training dropouts	1.9	1.4	0.1
Institutional completors	5.7*	1.3	16.5**
Institutional dropouts	6.8	2.2	0.3
Constant	39.4**	36.8**	108.7**
Standard error of estimate	19.4	11.6	44.0
Coefficient of determination[3]	0.49	0.46	0.36

*   Significant at the .05 level.

**   Significant at the .01 level.

1.   444 observations.

2.   This is the element of the set which enters the constant term.

3.   Adjusted for degrees of freedom.

example, that residents of Craven County received an average of $8.7 less in weekly earnings in the after-training period than residents of Richmond, Robeson and Scotland Counties, when the effects of prior labor force experience, physical handicaps, color, age, mobility, education, "drive", family status and training status are held constant.

The regression coefficients obtained by the use of the dummy variable technique outlined above are of course additive. To illustrate this point, we might make use of the data in Table 5 to estimate average weekly earnings for MITCE clients from Craven County who farmed before they entered training, had no physical handicaps, were white, aged 44 to 53, had never lived outside North Carolina since entering the labor force, had received 12 grades of schooling, had a low need-achievement rating, were males with no dependents, and had completed on-the-job training courses. The estimated average weekly earnings after training of these individuals would have been $39.4 - $8.7 - $11.2 + 0 + $14.5 - $8.1 + 0 + $14.0 - $3.0 + 0 + $11.6 = $48.5. By a similar process it can be shown that these individuals would have worked an average of 41.8 hours per week after training, for average hourly earnings of $1.02.

Finally, to use terms previously employed in Chapter II, where an element of an independent variable is associated with a significant change in net hours worked per week or net hourly wage rates in the after-training period, such influences will be referred to as *employment* and *wage* effects respectively.

RESULTS OF MULTIPLE REGRESSIONS:
COMPLETE CLASSIFICATION OF RESPONDENT TRAINING STATUS

In the initial regressions of our dependent variables (weekly earnings after training, hours worked per week after training and hourly earnings after training) on respondent characteristics, the training status of the respondent was classified according to whether he was a nontrainee, completed or dropped out of an on-the-job training course, or completed or dropped out of an institutional training course. When the number of independent variables used in these regressions is taken into account, the results shown in Table 5 are rather impressive. Most of the hypotheses used in selecting independent variables appear to be supported by the regression results.

The net difference in average earnings per week by area surprised the writer by its magnitude. The tri-county target area on the South Carolina border was the element dropped from this set. On net, respondents in Craven, Nash and Edgecombe Counties worked significantly fewer average hours per week for significantly lower average hourly pay rates. As a result, the average net weekly earnings of respondents located in Richmond, Robeson or Scotland Counties were $7.8 greater than the average net weekly earnings of respondents located in Nash and Edgecombe Counties. In similar fashion, location in Richmond, Robeson or Scotland Counties was associated with a net advantage in average weekly earnings of $8.7 over location in Craven County.

The prior labor force experience variable performed as had been anticipated. On net, former farmers did not work fewer hours per week in the after-training period than respondents who were employed in nonfarm jobs at the time they were first contacted by MITCE (the latter variable being the element dropped in this set), but the former farmers' average net hourly earnings were significantly lower in the after-training period. One of the more obvious explanations for this difference in earnings experience is that respondents who had farmed in the pre-training period were also likely to be farmers in the post-training period, and the returns to farm work are low.

Those respondents who were unemployed in the before-training period had significantly lower net average weekly earnings after training took place than respondents who were employed in the before-training period. Moreover, sample members who had been unemployed for 6 months or more at the time MITCE recruited for training had lower net average weekly earnings than sample members who had been unemployed for less than 6 months when MITCE recruited for training. However, sample members who considered themselves not to be in the labor force at the time they were first approached by MITCE had the lowest net average weekly earnings in the after-training period of all categories of respondents in the prior labor force experience set. But whereas the net earnings disadvantage of the formerly unemployed was attributable solely to the average number of hours worked per week, those respondents formerly not in the labor force experienced both adverse wage and employment effects in the after-training period.

The variable categorizing physical handicaps reveals a possible anomaly: the "moderately" handicapped having higher net average hourly earnings than respondents classified as not having any physical limitations at all. We may have assigned a few hypochondriacs to the former category: certainly the supposed ailments of these respondents (of which a full list was taken, providing a basis for subsequent classification) did not appear to affect their labor market performance adversely. There is little doubt, however, that our classification of the severely handicapped was correct: the net average weekly earnings of this category of respondents being $21 lower than the comparable earnings of respondents who were not handicapped at all.

Table 5 reveals that being white in North Carolina was associated with a net advantage of $14.5 in average weekly earnings. On net, the average number of hours worked per week by whites and nonwhites was not significantly different; the greater net average weekly earnings of whites were attributable to higher earnings levels per hour of work.

The regression coefficients in Table 5 indicate the existence of a nonlinear relationship between age and net average earnings levels. Respondents aged 21 to 33 years comprised the category of MITCE clients dropped in the age set, and there was no significant difference between their net average weekly earnings and the comparable earnings of respondents aged 34 to 43 years or under 21 years. This was another surprising result from the analysis. It had certainly been expected that workers under 21 years of age would have been at a greater disadvantage in the labor market.[14] However, there was a negative relation between net average weekly earnings and age in the case of more elderly MITCE clients. In the after-training period, the average net weekly earnings of respondents aged 44 - 53 years were more than $8 less than the comparable earnings of respondents aged 21 - 33, and the average net weekly earnings of respondents aged 54 years and older were nearly $16 less than the comparable earnings of respondents aged 21 - 33. The source of this decline in earnings with

_____

14. The regressions in fact revealed that workers under 21 years of age had a net average wage advantage of 10 cents an hour over respondents in the 21 to 33 years age bracket!

age is of interest. In the case of workers 54 years of age and older, it arose from a net decrease in both average hours worked per week and average hourly earnings. However, the net average hours worked per week by respondents in the 44 to 53 years age bracket were not significantly different from those worked by respondents aged 21 to 33; the source of the earnings disadvantage of the former age group being a lower net average hourly pay rate.

The "mobility" set regression coefficients reveal that those respondents who had lived in more than one state since joining the labor force had slightly higher net average weekly earnings than those respondents who had not lived outside North Carolina since joining the labor force. The small number of respondents who had lived in more than one state precluded testing the hypothesis that this variable was nonlinear in effect.

The education variable worked in the expected direction, increments of education above the eighth grade level being associated with successively higher net increases in average weekly earnings levels. The net increase in average weekly earnings associated with the completion of at least twelve grades of education was particularly marked, raising the question of whether the returns to the education of the high school graduates in our survey were attributable to "sheepskin effects".[15] As was noted in Chapter II, it is possible that earnings differentials may exaggerate productivity differentials between graduates and nongraduates, if employers use possession of a diploma or degree as a screening device to sift out job applicants with personality traits considered desirable in employees. The "sheepskin effect" hypothesis leads us to expect that this "bonus for graduation" would be mainly evident in differences in the employment rates of graduates and nongraduates, and it can be seen from Table 5 that those respondents who had completed at least 12 grades of education did, on net, work a significantly greater number of hours per week than MITCE clients with less education. However, it should be noted that the higher net average weekly earnings levels of respondents who had completed at least 12 grades of education were attributable more to higher earnings levels per hour of work than to working a greater number of hours per week.[16] It was argued in

---

15. It should be observed that completing at least 12 grades of education and graduating from high school are not necessarily synonymous events. It was possible to graduate from high school with an 11th grade education in North Carolina in earlier times, and this circumstance would have affected our older respondents.

16. This can be seen by using the net regression coefficients for the education set and the constant terms in the regression equations to construct alternative estimates of the average weekly earnings levels of MITCE clients. It will be recalled that the constant terms in the regression equations indicate the average weekly earnings, hours worked per week, and hourly earnings of respondents having characteristics which were dropped from the independent variable sets in running the regression equations. These respondents had 0-5 grades of education, and by multiplying the constant coefficients for hourly earnings and hours worked per week, it can be seen that they would have had average weekly earnings of $40.00 in the after-training period (108.7 cents per hour x 36.8 hours worked per week). If these respondents had instead completed at least 12 grades of education, the regression results indicate that they would have worked an average of 41.4 hours per week (36.8 + 4.6)

Chapter II that the productivity of a worker is best measured by his hourly wage rate. Accordingly, it was suggested that the allocative benefits from education or training programs should be defined as the increase in aggregate earnings levels associated with these investments in human capital, provided that such increases in aggregate earnings levels were in part attributable to significant increases in hourly earnings levels. Thus, by the standards adopted in the present study, the net increases in average weekly earnings associated with completing at least twelve grades of education represented genuine increases in the aggregate output of society and were not simply transfers of income from high school dropouts to high school graduates.

Turning to the family status set, the component of this variable referring to the sex of the respondent clearly had the largest impact on the explanatory power of the set as a whole. Nevertheless, the information coded on the presence and type of dependents also contributed to the explanatory power of the set. Thus the regressions reveal the interesting finding that the net average weekly earnings of women with dependents other than children were not significantly different from the net average weekly earnings of males with no dependents. With this exception, the family status set regression coefficients tend to support the hypotheses that women are at a disadvantage in the labor market, that family responsibilities (and especially children) create the incentive and the need for higher earnings levels, and that women with children in the house are hampered in the hours they can work.

An inspection of the coefficients in the need-achievement set shows that those respondents with low motivation had significantly lower net average weekly earnings than other respondents. The medium "drive" group was the element dropped in this set, and the net regression coefficient for the highest need-achievement group was not significant.

Finally, we come to the training status set. Nontrainee status comprised the element dropped in this set in running the regression equations. Considering the regression coefficients for the other categories of MITCE clients, the completion of on-the-job training was clearly associated with the largest increase in average earnings levels: the net average weekly earnings of MITCE clients who completed on-the-job training courses being $11.6 higher in the after-training period than the net average weekly earnings of nontrainees. The net average weekly earnings

---

for average hourly earnings of 127.2 cents (108.7 + 18.5). Multiplying these coefficients, we find that the average weekly earnings of those respondents having completed at least 12 grades of education would have been $52.66 in the after-training period, or $12.66 more than the average weekly earnings of those respondents having 0-5 grades of education. On the other hand, if the respondents having 0-5 grades of education in our example had worked the same number of hours per week in the after-training period as those respondents having completed at least 12 grades of education, their average weekly earnings would have been $45.00 (108.7 cents per hour x 41.4 hours worked per week). Thus in our example, the employment effect accounted for 39 per cent of the average increase in weekly earnings associated with completing at least 12 grades of education as compared to completing 0-5 grades of education. Similar calculations reveal that the employment effect accounted for 40 per cent of the average increase in weekly earnings associated with completing at least 12 grades of education as compared to completing 9-11 grades of education.

of MITCE clients who completed institutional training courses were also significantly greater than the corresponding earnings levels of nontrainees in the after-training period: the completion of an institutional training course being associated with a net increase in average weekly earnings of $5.7. The net average weekly earnings levels of MITCE clients who did not complete training courses were not significantly different from the corresponding earnings levels of nontrainees in the after-training period.

Turning to the regressions of the components of weekly earnings on respondent characteristics, it can be seen that of all the training categories, only the completion of on-the-job training was associated with significant employment effects: on-the-job training completors worked, on net, an average of 2.5 more hours per week in the after-training period than nontrainees. However, the completion of both on-the-job and institutional training were associated with significant wage effects. In the after-training period, the net average hourly earnings of on-the-job training completors were 25.4 cents greater than the net average hourly earnings of nontrainees, and the net average hourly earnings of institutional training completors were 16.5 cents greater than the net average hourly earnings of nontrainees.

The significant regression coefficients for the completion of training courses indicate the *absolute* differences between the net average earnings and employment levels of training completors and nontrainees in the after-training period. The earnings and employment levels of training completors can also be compared to those of nontrainees in *relative* terms, by dividing the respective regression coefficients by the constant terms for the regressions. Performing this manipulation, we find that in the after-training period the net average weekly earnings of on-the-job training completors were 29 per cent greater than the net average weekly earnings of nontrainees, and the net average weekly earnings of institutional training completors were 15 per cent greater than the net average weekly earnings of nontrainees. As noted above, training was only associated with significant employment effects for completors of on-the-job training courses. In the after-training period, net average hours worked per week by on-the-job training completors were only 7 per cent greater than the net average hours worked per week by nontrainees. However, the net average hourly earnings of on-the-job training completors and institutional training completors were respectively 23 per cent and 15 per cent greater after training than the net average hourly earnings of nontrainees.

How can we sum up our findings of the effects of training status on earnings in the after-training period? In the first place, it is clear that the net increases in average weekly earnings associated with the completion of training courses satisfy our rather stringent theoretical requirement for training to be shown to have allocative benefits; the main source of the net increase in average weekly earnings associated with completing on-the-job and institutional training courses being a wage effect which can properly be termed substantial. It was anticipated in Chapter II that average net hours worked per week by MITCE clients who completed on-the-job training courses would be somewhat greater than the average net hours worked per week by other MITCE trainees.[17] Table 5 revealed that the completion of on-the-job training was indeed associated with a positive employment effect, but roughly only one-fifth of the net increase in average weekly earnings associated with completing an on-the-job training course was attributable to working a greater number of hours per week.[18] The main source of the net increase in average weekly earnings for on-the-job training completors – and in the case of institutional training completors the only significant source of increased average weekly earnings – was a rise in net average hourly earnings levels after training.

Another interesting finding is that on-the-job training was associated with larger net increases in average weekly earnings for MITCE clients than institutional training. This matter will receive more attention in due course. It is also worth noting that the net average weekly earnings of training completors were significantly larger than the corresponding earnings levels of MITCE clients who failed to complete training courses. While the net average weekly earnings of both dropouts from on-the-job and institutional training were not significantly different from the corresponding earnings levels of nontrainees in the after-training period, we should note, however, that the number of institutional training dropouts was too small to expect any conclusive results from the regression analysis for this category of trainees.[19]

---

17. See Chapter II, footnote 22.

18. This can be seen by using the net regression coefficients for the training status set and the constant terms in the regression equations to construct alternative estimates of the average weekly earnings levels of MITCE clients. It will be recalled that the constant terms in the regression equations indicate the average weekly earnings, hours worked per week, and hourly earnings of respondents having characteristics which were dropped from the independent variable sets in running the regression equations. These respondents were nontrainees, and by multiplying the constant coefficients for hourly earnings and hours worked per week, it can be seen that they would have had average weekly earnings of $40.00 in the after-training period (108.7 cents per hour x 36.8 hours per week). If these respondents had instead completed on-the-job training courses, the regression results indicate that they would have worked an average of 39.3 hours per week (36.8 + 2.5) for average hourly earnings of 134.1 cents (108.7 + 25.4). Multiplying these coefficients, we find that the average weekly earnings of on-the-job training completors would have been $52.70 after training, or $12.70 more than the average weekly earnings of nontrainees. On the other hand, if the nontrainee respondents in our example had worked the same average number of hours per week in the after-training period as on-the-job training completors, their average weekly earnings would have been $42.72 (108.7 cents per hour x 39.3 hours worked per week). Thus in our example, the employment effect of completing on-the-job training therefore accounted for $2.72/$12.70 of the average increase in weekly earnings associated with completing an on-the-job training course, or roughly 21 per cent.

19. Our sample comprised 182 nontrainees, 131 on-the-job training completors, 51 on-the-job training dropouts, 61 institutional training completors and 19 institutional training dropouts.

RESULTS OF MULTIPLE REGRESSIONS:
SUMMARY CLASSIFICATIONS OF RESPONDENT TRAINING STATUS

Considerations of how the allocative benefits and costs of training programs should be calculated make it desirable to estimate the net average earnings increases associated with training for alternative classifications of the training status of MITCE clients to that employed in constructing Table 5. The discussion in Chapter II indicated that two basic classifications of *training status* have been employed in past analyses of the benefits and costs of training programs. In the first place, past analysts have often regarded the allocative benefits from training as being the increases in earnings associated with the training of individuals who completed their courses of instruction. If this reasoning is accepted — and pragmatically speaking, the results of Table 5 lend some credence to it — costs should also be computed on a "per-completor" basis in benefit-cost analyses of training schemes.[20] Table 5 has already reproduced the net earnings and employment regression coefficients associated with the completion of on-the-job and institutional training courses. To complement this approach, we need to find the net earnings and employment regression coefficients associated with the completion of all training sponsored by MITCE, irrespective of the particular type of training undertaken by the individual trainee. To this end, the regression equations used in constructing Table 5 were rerun with the training status set reclassified into three elements: nontrainees, training completors and training dropouts. The net earnings and employment regression coefficients associated with the completion of training courses are reproduced in Table 6.

The conclusion reached in Chapter II, however, was that the allocative benefits and costs of training programs should be compared on a "per-trainee" basis rather than on a "per-completor" basis. That is to say, the allocative benefits from training should be defined as the increases in earnings associated with the training of *all* participants in courses of instruction, and the allocative costs of training should be similarly defined. Where there are no increases in earnings levels associated with the training of dropouts, there should, of course, be no difference between allocative benefit-cost ratios for training programs calculated by either the per-trainee method or the per-completor method. However, our examination of the results of past benefit-cost analyses in Chapter II revealed that training may well be associated with increases in the earnings levels of individuals who fail to complete their courses of instruction.[21] As long as there is the possibility that the training of dropouts may be associated with increases in their earnings levels, it follows that the allocative benefits and costs of training programs should be calculated and compared on a per-trainee basis.

---

20. That is, if the allocative benefits from training to society are assumed to be the increases in earnings associated with the training of individuals who complete their courses of instruction, the allocative costs of training to society should be defined as the costs of training *all* participants in training programs, including those who fail to complete their courses of instruction.

21. See pp. 40-41 and footnote 39 in Chapter II.

Table 6: Multiple Regressions of Weekly Earnings after Training, and the Components of Weekly Earnings after Training, on Respondent Characteristics:

Summary Classifications of Training Status[1]

Training classification	Weekly earnings (dollars)				Hours worked per week				Hourly earnings (cents)			
	Regression coefficient	Regression constant	Se	$\bar{R}^2$	Regression coefficient	Regression constant	Se	$\bar{R}^2$	Regression coefficient	Regression constant	Se	$\bar{R}^2$
Training completors	10.2**	39.8**	19.4	0.49	2.3	36.8**	11.6	0.46	22.9**	108.9**	44.1	0.36
On-the-job trainees	8.8**	38.7**	19.8	0.48	2.2**	37.6**	11.7	0.45	19.6**	114.3**	44.7	0.35
Institutional trainees	5.9**	38.7**	19.8	0.48	1.6	37.6**	11.7	0.45	14.0**	114.3**	44.7	0.35
All trainees	8.3**	40.7**	19.5	0.48	2.1**	36.8**	11.6	0.46	17.2**	112.1**	44.5	0.35

** Significant at the .01 level.

$\bar{R}^2$ is the coefficient of determination adjusted for degrees of freedom.

Se is the standard error of estimate for the equation.

1. 444 observations.

The Benefits From Training

To compute the benefits from training MITCE clients on a per-trainee basis, it was necessary to rerun the regression equations used in constructing Table 5 with alternative classifications of the training status of MITCE clients. Two such sets of regressions were computed. In the first, MITCE clients were classified according to whether they were nontrainees, on-the-job trainees or institutional trainees. In the second, MITCE clients were simply classified according to whether they were trainees or nontrainees. The net earnings and employment coefficients from these regressions for on-the-job trainees, institutional trainees and all MITCE trainees are reproduced in Table 6.

It should be noted that the regression equations used in constructing Table 6 contained all of the independent variable sets used in constructing Table 5; only the training status set was altered, as specified above. As before, nontrainee status was the element dropped from the training status sets in the several regression equations. Thus Table 6 shows the amounts by which average earnings and employment figures for the various categories of trainees exceeded the comparable totals for nontrainees when the effects of geographical location, prior labor force experience, physical handicaps, color, age, mobility, education, need-achievement rating and family status are held constant.

RESULTS OF MULTIPLE REGRESSIONS:
SEPARATE REGRESSIONS FOR MALE AND FEMALE RESPONDENTS

In the course of the survey, one obtained the impression that the net change in average earnings levels associated with the training of MITCE clients varied markedly with the sex of the respondent. To test this hypothesis, separate regressions of earnings and employment on respondent characteristics were run for both male and female MITCE clients. This procedure of running separate regressions for men and women also has the advantage of providing a firmer basis for the projection of the allocative benefits from training. Such projections should allow for mortality rates over the working lifetime of respondents, and these mortality rates differ greatly by sex. Moreover, it should be realized that the regressions for women are important for other reasons. As was noted in Chapter I, previous benefit-cost analyses have not shown training to be particularly effective in raising the earnings of women.

Table 7 shows the net earnings and employment coefficients by sex for the various categories of trainees previously identified in Tables 5 and 6. Nontrainee status was, of course, the element dropped from the various training status sets in running the regressions. A sex set was substituted for the family status set in the regression equations used in constructing Table 7; otherwise, the same independent variable sets were used as in the estimating equations employed in constructing Tables 5 and 6.

It is clear that Table 7 contains results of major importance. To recapitulate, Tables 5 and 6 revealed that on-the-job training was associated with a greater net increase in the average weekly earnings of MITCE clients than

Table 7: Multiple Regressions of Weekly Earnings after Training, and the Components of Weekly Earnings after Training, on Respondent Characteristics:

Separate Regressions for Males and Females

	Weekly earnings (dollars)	Hours worked per week	Hourly earnings (cents)
MALES, COMPLETE CLASSIFICATION OF TRAINING STATUS[1]			
Net regression coefficients:			
OJT completors	9.5**	0.6	25.4**
OJT dropouts	0.7	1.9	- 1.1
Institutional completors	8.5**	1.9	25.0**
Institutional dropouts	8.1	2.9	15.0
Constant	56.9**	43.5**	139.2**
Standard error of estimate	21.3	11.2	45.3
Coefficient of determination[3]	0.33	0.28	0.33
MALES, SUMMARY CLASSIFICATION OF TRAINING STATUS[1]			
Net regression coefficients:			
All OJT trainees	7.4**	0.9	19.2**
All institutional trainees	8.3**	2.1	22.9**
Constant	57.0**	43.5**	139.3**
Standard error of estimate	21.4	11.2	45.8
Coefficient of determination[3]	0.32	0.28	0.31
FEMALES, COMPLETE CLASSIFICATION OF TRAINING STATUS[2]			
Net regression coefficients:			
OJT completors	17.0**	10.7**	22.4**
OJT dropouts	11.4**	4.0	10.2
Institutional completors	0.2	- 1.2	- 3.9
Institutional dropouts	- 3.2	- 1.8	-50.9**
Constant	21.8**	32.8**	63.6**
Standard error of estimate	14.2	11.5	38.0
Coefficient of determination[3]	0.42	0.44	0.32
FEMALES, SUMMARY CLASSIFICATIONS OF TRAINING STATUS[2]			
Net regression coefficients:			
All OJT trainees	14.5**	7.7**	17.6**
All institutional trainees	- 0.3	- 1.1	-12.4
Constant	22.1**	33.0**	65.7**
Standard error of estimate	14.2	11.5	38.3
Coefficient of determination[3]	0.42	0.44	0.31

** Significant at the .01 level.
OJT = on-the-job training.
1. 287 observations.
2. 157 observations.
3. Adjusted for degrees of freedom.

institutional training. Table 7 indicates that this finding was attributable to differences in the net change in the average weekly earnings of male and female MITCE clients associated with the two types of training.

There was really not much difference between the net change in average weekly earnings associated with on-the-job and institutional training for male MITCE clients. If we disregard completion status, institutional training was associated with slightly larger net increases in average weekly earnings than on-the-job training. On the other hand, the completion of on-the-job training was associated with slightly larger net increases in average weekly earnings than the completion of institutional training. Perhaps the most interesting aspect of the regressions for males was that neither on-the-job nor institutional training was associated with significant employment effects, although both forms of training were associated with significant wage effects.

When we turn to examine the net change in average earnings levels associated with the training of women, our findings are rather different. Institutional training seems to have been entirely useless as a method of raising the average net weekly earnings of women. By way of contrast, on-the-job training was associated with a net increase of $14.5 in the average weekly earnings of women. The net increase in average weekly earnings levels associated with on-the-job training for women was attributable to significant net increases in both the average number of hours worked per week and in average earnings levels per hour of work.

Table 7 also shows that net of the effects of other independent variables, the average weekly earnings of women who failed to complete on-the-job training courses were higher than those of female nontrainees, although not as high as the average weekly earnings of women who completed their on-the-job training. While it is true that this was the only instance in our analysis where training was associated with a significant net increase in the average weekly earnings of MITCE clients who failed to complete training courses, this finding does provide some necessary empirical backing for our earlier theoretical argument that benefits and costs should be calculated on a per-trainee basis in analyses of training schemes.

The poor results of institutional training for women deserve closer attention. They appear to be basically attributable to two factors: the choice of training occupations for the institutional classes and lack of motivation on the part of the trainees concerned. These factors will now be examined in turn.

Of those female institutional trainees who were interviewed, all but one were trained as nurse aides. Emphasis on training for this occupation both at the national MDTA level and in the MITCE project may have been misplaced. MDTA project officials are compelled by the MDTA Guidelines to concentrate training in "shortage" occupations.[22] There has been considerable debate in the

22.   See for instance *Manpower Administration Notice No. 3-66*, p. I-2.

economic literature concerning what exactly constitutes such a shortage occupation. A frequently accepted definition is that of Blank and Stigler:

> a shortage exists when the number of workers available (the supply) increases less rapidly than the number demanded at the salaries paid in the recent past. Then salaries will rise, and activities which once were performed by (say) engineers must now be performed by a class of workers who are less well trained and less expensive.[23]

The Department of Labor's guidelines as to what constitutes a shortage occupation are based on current market surveys and labor force projections.[24] The Department is well aware of some of the pitfalls in using these sources as a guide in deciding what training courses should be instituted. It acknowledges that some occupational shortages — that for nurse aides being specifically identified — are caused by low wage rates and wage rates that are not rising fast enough.[25] However, distinctions between "shortage" occupations and shortage occupations in which training is desirable tend to become blurred in some of the more brief instructions issued to the local MDTA project officials who are actually responsible for arranging institutional training classes and on-the-job training contracts.[26]

For obvious reasons, training for such low-wage occupations may not accomplish the official objectives of both directing labor into these occupations and raising the incomes of trainees. Trainees may complete their training and never proceed to use their skills in employment, because of the low wage levels obtaining in the jobs for which they were trained. For the same reason, trainees may quit such low-wage industries soon after entering them.[27]

---

23. David M. Blank and George J. Stigler, *The Demand and Supply of Scientific Personnel* (New York: National Bureau of Economic Research, 1957), p. 24.

24. See the *Manpower Report of the President for 1967,* Part III: "Occupational Shortages and Training Needs" (Washington, D.C.: Government Printing Office, 1967).

25. *"Inadequate pay and poor working conditions* are among the major causes of current personnel shortages in certain professions (teaching, social work, nursing) and service occupations (including nurse aides and other supporting occupations in hospitals and nursing homes)." *Manpower Report of the President for 1967,* p. 6 (original emphasis).

26. We note here the difference in the tone of the preceding footnote and the following direction in the 1967 MDTA Guidelines:

> It will be noted that certain categories which are acknowledged to be widely in short supply — cleaning and laundering occupations, food handling jobs, retail sales and other clerks, nurse aides and orderlies — are not included in the list of selected shortage occupations toward which roughly a third of MDTA resources are to be directed. *It is assumed nevertheless, that adequate training efforts will be made in these categories.*

Manpower Administration Notice No. 3-66, p. 1-7 (emphasis added).

27. In a recent paper Arthur Carol and Samuel Parry have attacked government training programs in low-wage occupations for reasons which abut on those mentioned in the text ("The Economic Rationale of Occupational Choice", *Industrial and Labor Relations Review* 21 (Jan., 1968): 183-96). It is worth noting that nurse aide training is also specifically criticized in their article. However, the argument of Carol and Parry contains

The Benefits From Training

Indeed, some fundamental questions have to be asked concerning the motivations of trainees who undertake training in these low-wage "shortage" occupations. The motivation of the women who enrolled in the nurse aide training sponsored by MITCE certainly contributed to the apparent failure of these institutional courses to raise the earnings of trainees, although it is debatable whether the motivational level of the trainees in these courses was solely a function of the occupation for which they were trained. Our interviews overwhelmingly revealed that most of these trainees were neither working nor looking for work before or after they took the training courses. A few clearly regarded this training as a kind of home science extension course: one said her nurse aide training helped in her occasional excursions into midwifery. This training may therefore have raised the nonmarket incomes of female MITCE clients, and it is clear that there may also have been third-party benefits from these nurse aide courses. Nevertheless, the alleged purpose of MDTA courses is to provide skills which the individual can use in employment. If our regression results contain a moral in this regard, it is that on-the-job training holds more promise than institutional training as a method of raising the earnings levels of women in the poverty population, because one can be more certain that a woman who undertakes on-the-job training is committed to the labor force.

RESULTS OF MULTIPLE REGRESSIONS:
SEPARATE REGRESSIONS
FOR DISADVANTAGED GROUPS OF MITCE CLIENTS

A secondary aim of our analysis was to establish whether training was associated with increases in the earnings of specific groups of MITCE clients considered to be disadvantaged in the labor market. We have already noted the effects on earnings associated with training one group which can properly be considered disadvantaged: that is, female MITCE clients. The MDTA Guidelines

---

elements not covered above. After calculating lifetime returns to training in 67 occupations, they conclude that

> Recent government training programs have been operating in a manner inconsistent with the policy implied by the foregoing. Given the educational background of the trainees and the cost of programs involved, training has not been for the highest-paying occupations. (*Ibid.,* p. 195.)

This charge requires substantiation: at present it "rests on unpublished U.S. Department of Labor data which show educational backgrounds of trainees by occupational training program" (*ibid.,* p. 195). Presumably, the conclusions of Carol and Parry also rest on their estimates of "normal" educational requirements in the occupations for which training took place. Some of the difficulties in estimating such "normal" educational requirements for occupations have already been noted in Chapter II.

The charge of Carol and Parry is serious not only because it implies that some of the education of participants in government training programs has been "unemployed", but also because the objective of making training available to "disadvantaged" groups in the labor force has been emphasized in all of these programs. Members of the labor force with little education constitute one such disadvantaged group. The charge of Carol and Parry, if valid, implies that more of the less educated could have been trained in these government programs.

specify that other such groups are to be given preference in admission to training programs. These disadvantaged groups include youths, nonwhites, persons with low academic achievement, the long-term unemployed,[28] older workers and family farm workers. Separate regressions of earnings and employment on respondent characteristics were run for *each* of these groups, and the results appear in Table 8.

In the regressions for these disadvantaged groups some changes were made in the format of the independent variable sets: changes dictated partly by the desire to preserve cell size and partly by the nature of the groups investigated. In all regressions, the family status set was discarded in favour of the sex set. In line with earlier reasoning, distinctions between dropouts and completors were also omitted in classifying training status. The training status categories distinguished were therefore nontrainees, institutional trainees and on-the-job trainees. In addition, because our intention was to determine whether training was associated with net increases in the average earnings levels of nonwhites, the white element was dropped from the color set in running the regressions (in Tables 5, 6 and 7, the reverse procedure was followed). Since the MDTA Guidelines define an "older worker" as anyone over 44 years of age,[29] our age categories were consolidated to reflect this classification. Likewise, a worker with anything less than 12 grades of education is considered in national MDTA to be at a disadvantage in the labor market.[30] MITCE clients in this educational category were reclassified into those with 8 or less grades of schooling, and those who left school after completing 9 to 11 grades.

Because of these changes in set format, care must be exercised in comparing the data in Table 8 with the data in earlier tables incorporating regression results. In particular, the constant terms in the Table 8 regressions bear little relation to the constant terms in earlier regression equations. However, the earnings and employment coefficients for the various training status groups in Table 8 bear the same interpretation as in previous tables. Nontrainee status was again the element dropped in each training status set in running the regressions. The other training status coefficients thus indicate the extent to which the net average earnings and employment levels of on-the-job and institutional trainees in the various disadvantaged groups differed from the comparable earnings and employment experience of nontrainees in the same disadvantaged groups.

To recapitulate on some earlier findings in our regression analysis, Table 6 revealed that on-the-job training was associated with a net increase of $8.8 in the

---

28. While the MDTA Guidelines actually define the long-term unemployed as those out of work for longer than 15 weeks, in order to preserve continuity with the classification system adopted in former regressions, the long-term unemployed will be defined below as those MITCE clients who were unemployed for more than 6 months in the before-training period.

29. See *Manpower Administration Notice No. 3-66*, p. 1-3.

30. *Ibid.*

Table 8: Multiple Regressions of Weekly Earnings after Training, and the Components of Weekly Earnings after Training, on Respondent Characteristics:

Separate Regressions for Disadvantaged MITCE Clients

Characteristic (No. of observations in brackets)	Weekly earnings (dollars)					Hours worked per week					Hourly earnings (cents)				
	OJT^1	$Inst.^2$	Constant	Se	$\bar{R}^2$	OJT	Inst.	Constant	Se	$\bar{R}^2$	OJT	Inst.	Constant	Se	$\bar{R}^2$
Labor force experience prior to training															
Farmer (96)	17.8**	14.7**	59.8**	21.7	0.36	4.1*	8.1**	32.6**	12.1	0.32	52.1**	29.4**	127.0**	46.1	0.37
Unemployed over 6 months (37)	10.1*	8.4	63.1**	15.3	0.55	4.3	-0.5	43.3**	8.6	0.66	6.0	34.1*	156.8**	30.0	0.45
Color															
Nonwhite (416)	8.9**	7.5**	67.8**	19.8	0.45	2.1*	2.1	47.9**	11.9	0.43	18.5**	16.1**	149.0**	44.6	0.33
Age as of 1 Jan., 1966															
44 years & over (95)	14.7**	7.8	62.7**	19.6	0.38	6.2**	7.3*	43.1**	12.5	0.46	24.8**	-3.2	108.5**	47.8	0.32
Under 21 years (79)	0.0	-8.8	80.5**	17.2	0.43	2.6	0.9	50.1**	10.4	0.29	-3.1	-19.0*	163.3**	32.8	0.30
Education															
0-8 grades (224)	13.0*	7.0*	65.5**	18.8	0.44	4.8**	4.0*	38.2**	12.1	0.41	24.4**	7.0	122.9**	41.0	0.34
9-11 grades (140)	11.0**	11.5**	66.9**	20.1	0.50	3.8*	0.2	50.3**	11.6	0.49	16.0*	33.7**	137.8**	52.9	0.32

*   Significant at the .05 level.

** Significant at the .01 level.

$\bar{R}^2$ is the coefficient of determination, adjusted for degrees of freedom.

Se is the standard error of estimate of the equation.

1. Net regression coefficient for on-the-job training.

2. Net regression coefficient for institutional training.

average weekly earnings of all MITCE clients. Similarly, institutional training was associated with a net increase of $5.9 in the average weekly earnings of all MITCE clients. All told, seven disadvantaged groups are distinguished in Table 8. For six of these groups, on-the-job training was associated with larger net increases in average weekly earnings than was on-the-job training for all MITCE clients. Three out of the seven net weekly earnings coefficients associated with institutional training for the disadvantaged groups were not significant. Nevertheless, the net weekly earnings coefficients associated with institutional training for the other four disadvantaged groups were larger than the net weekly earnings coefficient associated with institutional training for all MITCE clients. It is therefore fair to conclude that training proved to be more effective in raising the average weekly earnings levels of particular groups considered to be disadvantaged in the labor force than of the MITCE clientele in general. This finding is of some importance in its own right, and also because precisely the opposite conclusion is implied in at least one earlier benefit-cost analysis of MDTA-type training.[31]

The data in Table 8 also enable us to determine which of the two types of instruction sponsored by MITCE − on-the-job or institutional training − was associated with larger net increases in the average weekly earnings of the disadvantaged groups. Our earlier finding that on-the-job training was associated with larger net increases in the average weekly earnings of women applies to most of the other disadvantaged groups identified in Table 8, an exception being MITCE clients with 9 to 11 grades of education. Institutional training was, however, associated with significant net increases in the average weekly earnings of nonwhites, those who farmed in the pre-training period and those with 0-8 grades of education − although these net increases in average weekly earnings levels were not as large as those associated with on-the-job training for the same groups of MITCE clients.

A notable finding from the regressions for the disadvantaged groups is that neither on-the-job nor institutional training was associated with net increases in the average earnings levels of respondents under 21 years of age. There were no obvious reasons which would explain why training appeared to be ineffective as a means of increasing the average earnings levels of these MITCE clients; the writer confesses to being completely baffled by these results. In view of the importance attached in national MDTA to training for this age group, this problem merits further attention in future analyses of training schemes.

---

31.   For instance, Borus found that,

the older, less educated, or long-time unemployed worker would, on the average, have a lower probability of utilizing and benefiting from the retraining than would other workers who entered the course.

"Benefit-Cost Analysis of Retraining the Unemployed", pp. 391-92.

The Benefits From Training

RESULTS OF MULTIPLE REGRESSIONS:
RESPONDENT TRAINING STATUS
CLASSIFIED BY TRAINING OCCUPATION

As we have seen from the case of female institutional trainees, the occupation for which MITCE clients were trained was associated with net differences in their average earnings levels in the after-training period. A more systematic inquiry into the earnings and employment advantages associated with training for specific occupations was attempted in two final series of regressions. In the first series of regressions *all* MITCE trainees were classified according to the occupation for which they were trained. In the second series of regressions, only institutional trainees were classified according to the occupation for which they were trained. This distinction in the classification of MITCE clients by training occupation was frankly made in the belief that the official choice of institutional training occupations − other than the nurse aide course − might also reflect misjudgement of market conditions, whereas the private employers who participated in on-the-job training courses were less likely to make the same mistake. The two series of regressions also enable us to make some interesting inferences concerning the efficiency of on-the-job and institutional training in preparing MITCE clients for entry into particular occupations.

The earnings and employment coefficients associated with training for various occupations in the two series of regressions are reproduced in Table 9. The occupational classifications in Table 9 are broad and cover a variety of specific types of training.[32] In the set classifying all MITCE trainees by training occupation, nontrainees were represented by a dummy variable, and in the set classifying only institutional trainees by training occupation, nontrainees and on-the-job trainees were represented by separate dummy variables. In addition to the set classifying training status and training occupation, the regression equations used in constructing Table 9 contained the following independent variable sets: location, prior labor force experience, physical limitations, color, age, mobility, education, need-achievement status, and family status. The earnings and employment coefficients for each of the training occupations in Table 9 are net of the effects associated with the other independent variables

---

32. In the case of the *institutional* training courses, the contents of the "nurse aide" and "occupational farm tractor" courses are self-explanatory. The "miscellaneous" institutional training category included training for the occupations of sewing machine mechanic, heavy equipment mechanic, woodworking machine operator and electric appliance repairman. The institutional building trades courses covered the occupations of carpenter, bricklayer, welder, plumber and electrician.

In the case of the occupational classification for *all trainees,* the building trades category was similar in composition to the institutional classification. The "mechanic" classification covered much of the training already identified in the "miscellaneous" institutional training category, as well as a number of on-the-job clients trained to be auto mechanics. The "clerical and sales worker" training was confined to on-the-job training courses. The MITCE clients in the "service worker" category were trained mainly to be nurse aides or cooks. The residual "plant operative" category covered mostly on-the-job training courses in a variety of manufacturing industries.

−78−

Table 9: Multiple Regressions of Weekly Earnings after Training, and the Components of Weekly Earnings after Training, on Respondent Characteristics:

Training Status Classified by Training Occupation[1]

	Weekly earnings (dollars)	Hours worked per week	Hourly earnings (cents)
INSTITUTIONAL TRAINEES			
Net regression coefficients:			
Building tradesmen	12.9**	- 1.0	36.5**
Nurse aide	- 2.3	- 5.4*	- 8.7
"Occupational farm tractor"	0.3	3.9	5.3
Miscellaneous	14.4**	5.1*	26.3**
Constant	39.3**	36.9**	108.8**
Standard error of estimate	19.4	11.6	44.2
Coefficient of determination[2]	0.49	0.46	0.36
ALL TRAINEES			
Net regression coefficients:			
Clerical and sales workers	26.2**	8.2**	34.3**
Building tradesmen	10.5**	0.5	29.7**
Mechanics	6.7**	4.6**	10.0
Plant operatives	6.4**	1.6	15.7**
Service workers	- 0.1	- 1.5	- 7.0
Constant	40.5**	36.5**	111.2**
Standard error of estimate	19.4	11.6	44.3
Coefficient of determination[2]	0.49	0.46	0.36

*   Significant at the .05 level.

**   Significant at the .01 level.

1.   444 observations.

2.   Adjusted for degrees of freedom.

listed. In the set classifying training status and training occupation, nontrainee status was the element dropped in running the regressions. The coefficients in Table 9 therefore show the net amount by which the average weekly earnings, hours worked per week and hourly earnings of MITCE clients trained for various occupational categories differed from the comparable earnings and employment figures for nontrainees in the after-training period.

Table 9 reveals that the occupational training category associated with the greatest net increase in the average weekly earnings of MITCE clients was the clerical and sales worker category. However, it is doubtful whether a great deal can be concluded from this result. All but one of the MITCE clients who were trained for these occupations were females. These women clearly benefited from the training, but the size of the regression coefficient in this case probably also reflects the low alternative earnings of women nontrainees.

Most MITCE clients trained as building craftsmen were instructed in institutional training courses, and Table 9 shows that this form of training was associated with greater than average net increases in the weekly earnings of MITCE trainees. The "miscellaneous" category of institutional training, which was heavily weighted with the various mechanic courses, was associated with even larger net increases in the average weekly earnings of MITCE trainees. The fact that the weekly earnings coefficient associated with the "mechanic" occupational classification for all trainees was smaller than the weekly earnings coefficient for the "miscellaneous" institutional training category can perhaps be attributed to the on-the-job training contracts in this field. From what some of our respondents said, "training" was a misnomer for certain of these on-the-job training contracts. In particular, it appeared that respondents who were alleged to be getting instruction as auto mechanics were often nothing but gas station attendants.

Training for a variety of plant operative positions was associated with a moderate net weekly earnings advantage for MITCE clients. This training must be viewed in its proper context; much of it took place in the textile and furniture industries. These industries have traditionally been large employers in the North Carolina economy, although the textile plants at least have provided few jobs for nonwhites until recent years.[33] On-the-job training in these industries may therefore be regarded as a method of subsidizing entry for the predominantly nonwhite clientele of MITCE.

The fact that in the after-training period the average net weekly earnings of MITCE clients trained to be service workers were not significantly different from the average net weekly earnings of nontrainees can be attributed to the preponderance of nurse aide trainees in this training occupation category. The nurse aide training was not the only "failure" among the institutional courses: the

---

33. See for instance U.S., Equal Employment Opportunity Commission, *Negro Employment in the Textile Industries of North and South Carolina,* by Donald D. Osburn (Washington, D.C.: Equal Employment Opportunity Commission, 1966), pp. 12-33.

regressions show that another poor official choice of training occupation was the "occupational farm tractor" course. What the latter form of "training" conceivably achieved, of course, was to strengthen the attachment of the trainees concerned to farming. A primary aim of MITCE — for good reasons — was to ease the exit of its clients from the farming sector of the economy. MITCE's sponsorship of the "occupational farm tractor" course represents a curious departure from this objective.

SUMMARY OF FINDINGS IN THE REGRESSION ANALYSIS

Our analysis has by no means exhausted the information yielded by the survey data with a bearing on the allocative benefits from the training of MITCE clients. In particular, we have not studied the effects of the distance respondents had to travel to take training and of the period in the life of the MITCE project when their training occurred. However, these questions are slightly outside the main drift of the present chapter, and consideration of them is hence deferred to Appendix D.

The principal conclusion reached in this chapter is that the training sponsored by MITCE was associated with substantial increases in the average earnings levels of the project's clients. Net of the effects of the independent variables used in the regression analysis other than training status, the average weekly earnings of trainees were $8.3 greater than the average weekly earnings of nontrainees in the after-training period (the standard error of the net regression coefficient being $1.3).[34] The greater net average weekly earnings of trainees in the after-training period were attributable to the fact that trainees worked a net 2.3 hours more per week than nontrainees (0.8), and received a net average hourly wage 17.2 cents higher than that of nontrainees (2.9). Put another way, the net effect associated with training was an increase in the average earnings of MITCE clients by 20 per cent per week, due to a 6 per cent increase in average hours worked per week and a 15 per cent increase in average hourly wage rates. This large increase in average hourly wage rates is particularly important. It satisfies our criterion that for training to be shown to have allocative benefits, it should be associated with significant wage effects.

When we examined MITCE's training activities as a whole, it appeared we could infer that institutional training was markedly inferior to on-the-job training as a method of raising the net average weekly earnings levels of MITCE trainees. Further inquiry revealed that the demographic composition of the project's clientele and the occupations for which training took place influenced this result. Indeed, where rough comparisons could be made between on-the-job and institutional training *in particular skills,* institutional training appeared to be associated with greater net increases in the average weekly earnings levels of MITCE clients than on-the-job training.

---

34. Hereafter, standard errors will be given in parentheses following mention of a net regression coefficient.

The Benefits From Training

Unfortunately, several major blunders were made in the official choice of occupations for which training took place in institutional courses. This factor, taken together with the poor motivation of female institutional trainees, meant that institutional training appeared to be useless as a means of raising the net average weekly earnings of female respondents. By way of contrast, on-the-job training was associated with a net increase of $14.5 in the average weekly earnings of women (2.2). The net increase in average weekly earnings levels associated with on-the-job training for women was attributable to significant net increases in both the average number of hours worked per week and in average earnings levels per hour of work.

The net changes in average earnings and employment levels associated with the training of male MITCE clients were markedly different from the comparable changes in the earnings and employment levels of female MITCE clients. If training completion status is ignored, institutional training was associated with larger net increases in the average weekly earnings of males than on-the-job training. However, the margin of advantage was slight; institutional training was associated with a net increase in the average weekly earnings of males of $8.3 (2.7); on-the-job training was associated with a net increase in the average weekly earnings of males of $7.4 (1.8). Neither on-the-job nor institutional training were associated with significant employment effects for men; the net increases in average weekly earnings levels associated with both forms of training appeared to be entirely attributable to significant increases in the average hourly earnings levels of male trainees.

All things considered, the training sponsored by MITCE was associated with larger net increases in the average weekly earnings levels of specific groups considered to be disadvantaged in the labor force than of the MITCE clientele in general. Moreover, in the case of the MITCE clients who had characteristics considered to convey disadvantages in the labor force, on-the-job training was associated with greater net increases in average weekly earnings levels than institutional training. An interesting finding from the regression analysis for disadvantaged groups of MITCE clients was that both on-the-job and institutional training appeared to be ineffective as means of increasing the average weekly earnings of respondents under 21 years of age. This matter should be a focus for further research.

So far we have established the extent to which training was associated with increases in the weekly earnings levels of MITCE clients during a period averaging 16 months after they finished their training. This information provides us with the means of estimating the total allocative benefits from training — including allocative benefits which accrued after our survey period. The data from our regressions also enable us to infer whether the training sponsored by MITCE satisfied the distributional objectives of the antipoverty program. The tasks of estimating the total allocative effects of the MITCE project, and of assessing the distributional effects of training, will be undertaken in Chapter IV.

CHAPTER IV

THE MITCE PROJECT AS JUDGED BY EFFICIENCY AND DISTRIBUTIONAL INVESTMENT CRITERIA

It was proposed in Chapter I that the success of Manpower Improvement through Community Effort be assessed in terms of the "distributional" and "allocative" effects of the project. The present chapter will bring together the information needed to reach judgements on the basis of these criteria.

In the light of our previous findings, assessment of the distributional effectiveness of the training activities of MITCE is considered to be the less urgent of the two tasks confronting us. The regression analysis of Chapter III indicated that the overall MITCE training program was associated, in the survey period, with a net increase of 20 per cent in the average weekly earnings of MITCE clients. Moreover, if the intercept terms from the regressions of weekly earnings on respondent characteristics are regarded as rough indicators of the modal earnings levels of MITCE clients, there is very little doubt that without training most of the MITCE clientele would have been considered part of the poverty population. It thus appears likely that the MITCE project satisfies what was considered in Chapter II to be the minimum condition of acceptability for an antipoverty program: that it should raise the incomes of the poor. However, this and other issues involved in assessing the distributional effectiveness of the MITCE project will be examined with greater precision later in this chapter.

Assessment of MITCE from an "allocative" or "efficiency" standpoint involves determining whether the project's overall training activities raised the aggregate output of society by more than the allocative costs of training to society. As was indicated in Chapter II, if a training program raises the incomes of the poor and has an allocative benefit-cost ratio at least equal to unity, it will represent a desirable method of reducing poverty to society. Such a program outcome indicates that society has not had to make any sacrifices in total output in the process of raising the incomes of the poor. In view of the importance of the "efficiency" criterion in assessments of an antipoverty project, the first section of this chapter will be devoted to the preparation of allocative benefit-cost ratios for MITCE.

Our application of the efficiency and distributional criteria will not be limited to assessment of the total MITCE program. Subsidiary aims of our analysis have been to compare the effectiveness to society of training men as against training women and to compare the effectiveness to society of the two forms of skill instruction offered by MITCE – on-the-job and institutional training. The same efficiency and distributional criteria will be employed in answering these questions. Our task is therefore to prepare benefit-cost ratios and data on the distribution of increases in earnings associated with training for all MITCE trainees and separately for male on-the-job trainees, female on-the-job trainees and male institutional trainees. There is, of course, no point in performing the computations for female institutional trainees, since the regressions in Chapter III revealed that on average there was no increase in earnings levels associated with training these MITCE clients. However, we should resist the temptation of inferring that there were no distributional or allocative benefits from the nurse aide courses in which these female MITCE clients were enrolled. It was indicated in Chapter III that this training may have raised the nonmarket output of trainees, and we have not attempted to value any such increases in nonmarket output which may be associated with training.

THE ALLOCATIVE BENEFITS TO SOCIETY FROM TRAINING

In calculating the "present value" of the allocative benefits from training, a modified version of a formula employed by Miller and Hornseth[1] was used.

$$Va = \sum_{N=A}^{64} \frac{YaPn (1 + X)^{N-A+\frac{1}{2}}}{(1 + R)^{N-A+1}}$$

Where: Va = the present value of all allocative training benefits from age A – the average age of the respondents at the end of training – through age 64.

Ya = the annual increase in earnings associated with training in the survey period.

Pn = the number of survivors at age N.

R = the rate of discount used to convert future earnings to their present values.

X = the annual increase in earnings levels due to rising productivity.

There are many issues involved in the choice of values for this formula which require closer examination. The components of the formula will therefore be discussed in the approximate order listed above.

---

1.   U.S., Department of Commerce, Bureau of the Census, *Present Value of Estimated Lifetime Earnings,* by Herman P. Miller and Richard A. Hornseth, Technical Paper No. 16 (Washington, D.C.: Government Printing Office, 1967), p.2.

The Ages and Projected Mortality Rates of MITCE Trainees

The average age of male on-the-job trainees, female on-the-job trainees and all MITCE trainees was 32 years at the end of training. It was assumed, following the conventional practice, that the normal retirement age of trainees would be 65 years. Of course, in projecting the benefits to training over the interval between 32 or 34 years and 65 years, we have to allow for the possibility of death before age 65. The nonwhite sections of 1964 life tables for the United States were used to make this adjustment, since our sample was largely nonwhite in composition.[2]

The Annual Allocative Benefits from Training in the Survey Period

In accordance with the analysis in Chapter II, the allocative benefits from training in the survey period were considered to be the increases in aggregate earnings levels associated with training, provided that such increases in aggregate earnings levels were in part attributable to significant increases in hourly earnings levels. The regression analysis in Chapter III revealed that the earnings increases associated with on-the-job training for males and females, institutional training for males, and training for MITCE clients considered collectively were indeed made up to a significant extent of wage effects. The net weekly earnings regression coefficients associated with the training of these categories of MITCE clients were therefore recomputed on an annual basis for use in the formula to obtain the total allocative benefits from training. This procedure yielded annual allocative benefits in the survey period − in order of magnitude − of $756 for each female on-the-job trainee, $433 for each MITCE trainee, $429 for each male institutional trainee and $384 for each male on-the-job trainee.

However, the regression analysis in Chapter III disclosed that for some categories of MITCE clients, the increases in earnings associated with training were partly attributable to significant increases in employment. Some researchers would not consider the increases in the earnings levels of trainees which were attributable to such employment effects to be genuine allocative benefits to society. For instance, Morgan and David have calculated the rate of return to education on the basis of what annual earnings levels would be if members of the labor force worked for the same number of hours per year at *prevailing* hourly wage levels. If the criteria of Morgan and David were adopted in our analysis, we would assume that all MITCE clients worked 2000 hours per

---

2.   U.S., Department of Health, Education and Welfare, Public Health Service, *Vital Statistics of the United States, 1964,* vol. II, *Mortality* (Washington, D.C.: Government Printing Office, 1966), p. 5-5.

These life tables forcibly remind us of some of the consequences of race and poverty. As noted above, the average age of trainees in our sample was 32 years at the end of training. The probability of a person of this age surviving to be 65 years old is as follows:

White females	−	84 per cent
White males	−	70 per cent
Nonwhite females	−	66 per cent
Nonwhite males	−	56 per cent

year and that the annual allocative benefits from training in the survey period were 2000 times the increases in hourly earnings associated with training. Although this more stringent basis for calculating the allocative benefits from training was rejected for use in our analysis, Appendix E indicates how the allocative benefits and benefit-cost ratios for the training sponsored by MITCE would be affected if the criteria of Morgan and David had been adopted.

The Social Discount Rate

Society is not indifferent to the time-profile of training benefits: a dollar in benefits today is obviously of greater value to us than a dollar of benefits in 30 years time. In order to measure the benefits and costs from MITCE's training activities on a comparable basis, we therefore have to find the discounted value of benefits at the time when training costs were incurred.

Efficiency in the allocation of national resources requires that the social discount rate used in assessing public investment programs be equal to the opportunity cost of withdrawing resources from the private sector of the economy. Several different approaches have been taken in calculating this social opportunity cost of public funds. Nevertheless, a majority of academic economists testifying before Joint Economic Committee Hearings in 1967-68 concurred that 10 per cent was an appropriate figure for the social opportunity cost of public funds.[3] Social opportunity cost considerations have also led the Bureau of the Budget to advocate the adoption of a 10 per cent social discount rate in issuing guidelines for discounting procedures to federal agencies.[4] For the same reason, a 10 per cent social discount rate is applied uniformly throughout the Department of Defense in evaluating expenditures "where the sole or

---

3.   In the 1967 Joint Economic Committee Hearings, William Baumol, Jacob Stockfisch and Morton Kamien agreed that 10 per cent was a suitable social discount rate on opportunity cost grounds. It should, however, be noted that Stockfisch was of the opinion that the opportunity cost of public funds was between 10 and 15 per cent, but concurred in the use of 10 per cent as a social discount rate on the grounds that higher rates would make little difference to the valuation of long-lived capital projects. In addition, Kamien thought that a social discount rate of 10 per cent might need to be adjusted downward to allow for the incorporation of inflationary expectations in the cost of public funds. The latter point will be considered at greater length below. U.S., Congress, Joint Economic Committee, Subcommittee on Economy in Government, *The Planning − Programming − Budgeting System: Progress and Potentials, Hearings,* 90th Cong., 1st sess., 1967, pp. 160, 161 and 166-67. For another presentation of Baumol's views, see his article, "On the Social Rate of Discount", *American Economic Review* 58 (Sept., 1968): 793.

In the 1968 Joint Economic Committee Hearings, Otto Eckstein and Arnold C. Harberger also testified on this issue. Eckstein thought that the social opportunity cost of public funds was 8 per cent and advocated the adoption of a social discount rate of 7 - 7½ per cent for reasons that were not specified. Harberger was of the opinion that the correct social discount rate on opportunity cost grounds was 10.7 per cent, and that further research would be unlikely to modify this estimate by more than 2 per cent: i.e. the figure ultimately arrived at would be between 8.7 and 12.7 per cent. U.S., Congress, Joint Economic Committee, Subcommittee on Economy in Government, *Economic Analysis of Public Investment Decisions: Interest Rate Policy and Discounting Analysis, Hearings,* 90th Cong., 2nd sess., 1968, pp. 56 and 65.

4.   Joint Economic Committee, *Hearings on Interest Rate Policy and Discounting Analysis,* p. 28.

primary justification for such projects is economic".[5] Accordingly, a social discount rate of 10 per cent will be employed in the text to derive the present value of benefits from training.

However, despite the above evidence, it should be made clear that there are still substantial differences of opinion concerning the exact size of the correct social discount rate. Given these differences of opinion, it is appropriate to test the sensitivity of the present value of training benefits to discount rates other than 10 per cent. Mostly in order to represent fairly the range of opinion expressed by academic economists at the Joint Economic Committee Hearings in 1967-68, rates of 8 and 12 per cent were selected for this purpose. Present values of training benefits calculated on the basis of these alternative social discount rates are reproduced in Appendix E.

Testing the sensitivity of the present value of benefits to alternative discount rates may be an appropriate procedure for another reason. It is evident that little attention has been paid to the important question of whether estimates of the social discount rate should be expressed gross or net of expectations of future price movements. Since the approach employed in a number of past estimates of the social discount rate has been to calculate the total social cost of current government borrowing including the actual interest charges on newly issued debt, and since interest costs certainly reflect expectations of future price movements, it is clear that calculations of the social discount rate can also be influenced by expectations of future price movements. Owing to linkages in the capital market, one would expect estimates of the social discount rate constructed on alternative bases — such as the social opportunity cost of tax-raised government funds — to be similarly influenced by expectations of future price movements.

Recognition of this fact implies that one of two procedures should be adopted in benefit-cost evaluation of public investment projects where benefits accrue or costs are incurred over different time periods. On the one hand a "real" social discount rate (i.e., one that is net of any expectations of future price movements) could be employed to compare benefits and costs estimated in constant dollar values. The alternative procedure is to use a social discount rate which incorporates expectations of future price movements, and simultaneously to adjust all benefits and costs in the analysis to allow for future price movements. The former procedure has been adopted in principle in the present analysis. This procedure has some rational appeal in that it would seem to make more sense to alter one price in the analysis than all prices but one.

The question that immediately arises from the decision to adopt the use of a "real" social discount rate in the present analysis is whether the actual rates employed were constructed on this basis. A perusal of the testimony at the Joint Economic Committee Hearings, from which our rates were principally chosen,

5. *Ibid.,* p. 146.

indicates that while most witnesses were aware of the problem being discussed, there was little concrete testimony on the issue of how much effect expectations of future price movements would have on the social discount rate. A generous interpretation of this testimony would be that in those cases where the estimates of the social discount rate were admitted to be affected by expectations of price movements, the witnesses concerned thought that social discount rates net of such price influences would not differ greatly from the corresponding "gross" estimates.[6] It is on this rather tenuous basis that the decision was made not to alter the social discount rates chosen for use in the present analysis to allow for expectations of future price movements. However, our use of a spread of rates in deriving the present value of training benefits in Appendix E may remedy the deficiences inherent in reliance on any single social discount rate.

The Secular Rate of Growth in Real Earnings

As Houthakker has noted,

> in a growing economy every individual may expect an upward pattern in his own earnings superimposed on the cross-sectional pattern for a given year.[7]

Accordingly, in projections of real earnings levels based on cross-section study findings we should make allowances for the effects of rising national productivity over time. However, Becker has pointed out that in calculating the rate of return to investments in the quality of the labor force — such as education and training programs — we should not adjust future earnings levels by the *total* estimated growth rate in per capita earnings levels, since part of the estimated growth in future earnings levels will itself be attributable to such increases in the quality of the labor force. Based on Denison's findings for the period 1929-57, Becker reduced the per capita rate of growth of output by 25 per cent to allow for this factor in his own estimates of the rate of return from education.[8]

Our own estimates of the future growth of earnings for a labor force of "constant quality" were based on experience in the years 1950-65, when the

---

6. Thus it was Eckstein's estimate that under 1968 conditions —

> I do not think one can justify a large further decline in the assumption about the interest rate from the present levels. You could argue for a fall of another quarter of a per cent or a half a per cent as wartime circumstances and the current inflation. [*sic*] But that seems to me what the most prudent man would project.

Hearings on Interest Rate Policy and Discounting Analysis, p. 71. This may in fact be why Eckstein advocated use of a social discount rate of 7 - 7½ per cent at the same time as he estimated the social opportunity cost of public funds to be 8 per cent. *Ibid.*, p. 56. It should be noted that Eckstein's view of the effects of inflationary expectations on recent interest rates differs substantially from other findings on this issue. See William P. Yohe and Denis S. Karnosky, "Interest Rates and Price Level Changes, 1952-69", *Federal Reserve Bank of St. Louis Review* 51 (Dec., 1969): 18-38.

7. H. S. Houthakker, "Education and Income", *Review of Economics and Statistics* 41 (Feb., 1959): 27.

8. *Human Capital*, p. 73.

annual rate of growth of output per employee was 2.4 per cent.[9] According to Griliches, it is still appropriate to reduce the rate of growth of output per member of the labor force in the post-World War II period by 25 per cent to allow for increases in the quality of the labor force.[10] On these grounds, a growth rate of 1.8 per cent was chosen for use in the projections of our analysis as reflecting the likely annual growth in earnings to a labor force of constant quality.[11]

However, it must be acknowledged that considerable uncertainty surrounds the relationship between future growth and earnings levels. Under the circumstances, it is perhaps appropriate to follow Becker's example and test the sensitivity of our projections of earnings for annual growth rates of 0, 1 and 2 per cent. The results of such a sensitivity analysis are presented in Appendix E.

The Total Allocative Benefits from Training

After making all of the adjustments described above, the present value of the allocative benefits associated with training — in order of magnitude — were $8,113 for female on-the-job trainees, $4,623 for all MITCE trainees, $4,396 for male institutional trainees and $4,014 for male on-the-job trainees.

THE ALLOCATIVE COSTS OF TRAINING

Two components of training costs will be distinguished in the subsequent analysis. On the one hand, there are the costs of hiring factors in connection with the training process — the costs of personnel, materials and plant and equipment. These costs will be analyzed further in terms of expenditures financed under the MITCE contract for activities such as recruiting and counselling trainees, and finding employment for graduates of training programs: the "direct" costs of training associated with the day-to-day operation of

---

9.   U.S., Department of Commerce, Bureau of the Census, *Long Term Economic Growth* (Washington, D.C.: Government Printing Office, 1966), p. 101. The period 1950-65 was chosen as the base for extrapolation of future productivity growth because this was the longest series confined to the years since World War II for which growth rates in output per employee were calculated in *Long Term Economic Growth*. On the one hand, growth experience in the years since World War II was presumed to be more relevant as a basis for projecting future growth rates than growth experience in periods extending further back in time. Annual growth rates for periods which encompass the Great Depression or the early years of the Twentieth Century are of course lower than that for the period 1950-65. Thus, the annual growth rate in output per employee was 1.5 per cent in the period 1909-65 and 1.8 per cent in the period 1929-65 *(Ibid.,* p. 101 and calculated from the data on p. 188). On the other hand, it should be noted that the choice of a base period which emphasized more recent growth experience than in 1950-65 would have led to higher projections of the rate of growth of output per employee. For instance, in the period 1960-65, the annual rate of growth of output per employee was 3.1 per cent *(Ibid.,* p. 101).

10.   For the data on which this conclusion is based, see Zvi Griliches, "Notes on the Role of Education in Production Functions and Growth Accounting", in *Education, Income and Human Capital*, ed. W. Lee Hansen (New York: National Bureau of Economic Research, 1970), p. 79.

11.   For similar calculations of the future annual growth in earnings to a labor force of constant quality, see Glen G. Cain, *Benefit-Cost Estimates for Job Corps,* pp. 41-42.

on-the-job and institutional courses; and the "indirect" costs incurred by Federal and State agencies in supervising and administering training programs. In a separate category we will distinguish the costs of the output loss to society because MITCE clients were in training when they might have been contributing to output. Although only the latter category of costs will be referred to as "opportunity costs", it was noted in Chapter II that *all* of the costs of training to society — irrespective of category — can be viewed in this light.

MITCE Expenditures

MITCE was not *directly* engaged in training its clients. MITCE personnel recruited workers for on-the-job and institutional training, checked their progress during training, and attempted to find jobs for them when they had completed their training. The costs of these functions performed by the MITCE staff were therefore of an "overhead" nature in relation to the training process.

Total expenditures during MITCE's first contract with the Department of Labor — the period covered by this study — amounted to $902,183. However, not all of these costs should be charged against the training of workers under the first contract of MITCE. In the first place, some of these expenditures should be viewed as "initial costs" required to establish the project on a working basis. Such expenditures would include those incurred in organizing target area offices, in training project personnel, in the initial canvass of the population in the target areas, and in the necessary coordination with State and Federal officials to inaugurate courses for MITCE clients. Since these initial costs obviously lowered subsequent expenditures incurred in training MITCE clients, it is only reasonable that they be spread over both of the project's contracts with the Department of Labor. Such an allowance was made by taking all expenditures incurred from the inception of the project through October 31, 1965, and the costs of a subsequent training session for all project personnel in January, 1966, and allocating one-half of such costs to each of the project's contracts. The cut-off point of October, 1965 was selected on the grounds that a critical staff conference occurred immediately before this date. This conference led to virtual reorganization of the project, and its effects were immediately noticeable in the volume of trainees recruited.[12]

Making the suggested alteration lowers total costs under the first MITCE contract to $723,238. However, there is still some doubt as to whether the whole of this adjusted sum of expenditures should be charged against the training of workers under the first contract of MITCE. Much of the time of the project's personnel and considerable expenditures were consumed in providing services to persons who did not subsequently enter training courses. The

---

12. "At the end of the July-August reporting period only 25 persons had been placed on B.A.T. approved on-the-job training programs [and] six persons into institutional training programs. In view of this, recruitment was stopped and a training session was held in October, 1965. . . . The team system was established [here]. The team system proved effective as an organized approach to problem finding and solving." *MITCE Final Report*, pp. 17-18.

provision of these services to nontrainees was justifiable under the terms of the original MITCE contract,[13] but the question of concern to the present analysis is whether the benefits and costs of these nontraining activities of MITCE should be evaluated separately from the training functions of the project. It was eventually decided that it would not be valid to differentiate between the activities of the project in this way, since in the opinion of senior MITCE personnel the provision of services to nontrainees was an inseparable and inescapable cost of recruiting and preparing clients for training. Accordingly, the "overhead" cost for each trainee arising from activities financed by MITCE's first contract was taken to be $1,106, or $723,238 divided by the 654 MITCE clients who were trained during the course of the project's first contract.

A rather broader issue is raised in considering the services MITCE extended to nontrainees. We should recall that MITCE was an MDTA Experimental and Demonstration Program; its specific objective was to see how training could best be used to raise the incomes of a population which was severely handicapped in the labor market. The services MITCE extended to nontrainees are perhaps best viewed as part of the costs of the experimental activities of the project. It is not possible to distinguish all of the costs of MITCE's experimental activities on any realistic basis, and we have in fact treated all MITCE contract costs, other than "initial" costs, as being current operational costs. By dealing with MITCE's costs in this manner, we are imparting a downward bias to the benefit-cost ratios for the training activities of the project, since there is little doubt that costs per trainee would be lower in regular MDTA training programs which do not have experimental objectives.

The Direct Course Costs of Institutional Training

Respondents in our survey of MITCE clients who were institutional trainees had been enrolled in 15 different training courses, all but four of which had been audited when our study was instituted. For the courses which had been audited, a breakdown of direct costs was available from Form OE-4000 of the Department of Health, Education and Welfare. These direct costs cover such items as salaries of instructors, materials used in the courses, fixed charges,[14] expenditures to maintain and repair equipment, expenditures incurred in purchasing equipment and any minor plant remodelling necessary for the courses, and other costs such as janitorial services. For the courses which had not

---

13. According to the first contract of MITCE with the U.S. Department of Labor, an ancillary aim of the project was to demonstrate that

in the course of operating a manpower program, all of the people in the rural target area who are in need of available services can be aided to some degree. In the course of searching for those individuals who can be aided by other existing programs, this project will secure the cooperation of other agencies so that the project can refer those in need to these programs.

MITCE Final Report, p. 4.

14. These were mainly government contributions to fringe benefit plans for personnel employed in running the courses.

been audited, average direct cost figures were obtained on an aggregate basis from the North Carolina Department of Community Colleges.

Some reservations were held concerning the inclusion of all direct costs as officially compiled in our cost estimates. In the first place, the purchase of equipment and alterations to the Community College plants constituted an average of over 9 per cent of direct costs in all audited courses. The inclusion of all of these costs overstates the cost of training MITCE clients, since this capital equipment and the altered facilities of the Community Colleges would subsequently be used by trainees in other MDTA courses and even trainees not connected with MDTA. In a thorough accounting of course costs, only actual user costs would be charged against the training of MITCE clients.

However, the direct costs of training as reported to the Department of Health, Education and Welfare do not make any allowance for another item of user costs: namely, the opportunity cost of the North Carolina Community College facilities involved in MDTA training. Owing to lack of information concerning the alternative value of the public facilities used in these courses, no attempt was made to estimate such costs. It was assumed that the effect of this omission would be balanced by the decision to include the total costs of equipment purchase and plant remodelling for the courses.

There are some grounds for arguing that our calculations of direct course costs still overstate the costs of institutional training for MITCE clients. Only three of the classes attended by our respondents were arranged by the Employment Security Commission of North Carolina *specifically* for MITCE clients. On the other hand, MITCE was often asked at short notice by the State authorities to obtain recruits from among its clients for other institutional training courses. Since the courses which were not arranged specifically for MITCE clients would have proceeded in their absence, the marginal instruction costs of training MITCE clients in the latter courses would be limited to a few small items such as the value of materials used. All other costs would have been incurred anyway. Thus in some ways our estimates of direct course costs − $445 for each institutional trainee and $546 for each male institutional trainee[15] − may be overestimates of the actual marginal costs.

The Opportunity Costs of Institutional Trainees

Society also incurred costs in the form of forgone output while MITCE clients were participating in institutional training courses. This loss can be valued by estimating what trainees would have earned had they not been in training, and deducting from this sum any trainee earnings from part-time employment during the institutional training courses.

---

15. Costs per institutional trainee were calculated solely for the purpose of subsequently estimating the costs of training *all* MITCE clients.

To estimate the "alternative" earnings of trainees, a regression was run for nontrainees with weekly income during the training period as the dependent variable. The independent variable sets used in the regression equation accounted for the effects of geographical location, prior labor force experience, physical handicaps, color, age, mobility, education, need-achievement status and family status.[16] The regression coefficients for the various elements of the sets were then weighted by the proportion of institutional trainees having the characteristics in question. By this procedure it was estimated that all institutional trainees would have had average weekly earnings of $25.6 during the training period had they not been in training, and male institutional trainees considered separately would have had weekly earnings of $31.2. Taking into account the fact that all institutional trainees spent 22.0 weeks in training and male institutional trainees spent 27.1 weeks in training, total "alternative" earnings were roughly $563 for each institutional trainee and $846 for each male institutional trainee. However, some trainees contributed to output by obtaining part-time employment during training. These earnings amounted to an average of approximately $47 for each institutional trainee and $55 for each male institutional trainee. The true opportunity cost of institutional training to society in terms of the forgone output of trainees was therefore — allowing for rounding — $516 for each trainee and $791 for each male trainee.

The Direct Course Costs and Opportunity Costs
of On-the-Job Training

As noted in Chapter II, the only direct course costs incurred by the federal government in connection with on-the-job training for MITCE clients were subsidies to employers averaging $68 for each female MITCE trainee and $108 for each male MITCE trainee. The opportunity costs of on-the-job trainees, like the opportunity costs of institutional trainees, are the wages forgone by individuals during the period of instruction. Consequently, the wages on-the-job trainees would have earned had they not been in training were estimated by the method adopted in finding the opportunity costs of MITCE institutional trainees. These estimates revealed that the "expected" hourly wages of male and female on-the-job trainees if they had not been in training would have been below the legal minimum-wage levels employers were required to pay during the training period. It was therefore concluded that MITCE trainees incurred no opportunity costs while receiving on-the-job training, and that the federal subsidies provided to employers undertaking on-the-job training contracts partly represented a reimbursement for administering a transfer payment. In view of the comparatively minor sums involved, it was not felt worthwhile to make further enquiries as to what proportion of these subsidies represented allocative costs to society and what proportion represented transfer payments to trainees.

---

16. The regression equation was thus similar in all respects to that used in Table 5, except that the training status set was dropped. The method used in simulating the alternative earnings of institutional trainees is analogous to that employed in the illustration on pp. 61-62.

The Mitce Project

Our treatment of these subsidies to employers as being allocative costs to society will consequently represent an over-estimate of the resources forgone by society because MITCE clients were trained on-the-job.

The "Indirect" Costs of Training

An allowance has also to be made for costs incurred by the Federal Government in the administration and supervision of on-the-job and institutional training at the Federal and State levels. These functions are performed by the Bureau of Employment Security and the Bureau of Apprenticeship and Training of the Department of Labor, and the Office of Education of the Department of Health, Education and Welfare. Following the practice suggested by the Planning Research Corporation, the expenditures necessary to provide these support functions for the average MDTA trainee were first calculated on a weekly basis.[17] When this "weekly factor" cost was multiplied by the number of weeks MITCE clients were in training, it was found that average indirect costs were $13 for each female on-the-job trainee, $21 for each male on-the-job trainee, $70 for each institutional trainee, and $87 for each male institutional trainee. The arithmetic underlying these calculations is shown in Tables 10 and 11.[18]

The Total Allocative Costs of Training

The various components of the allocative costs of training are aggregated in Table 12. It should be noted that the cost calculations for all institutional trainees are included in Table 12 solely because a benefit-cost ratio will subsequently be calculated in Table 13 for the training of all MITCE clients. In the latter calculation, costs for each trainee will be derived by weighting on-the-job and institutional training costs according to the numbers of each type of trainee in our sample.

THE ALLOCATIVE BENEFIT-COST RATIO FROM TRAINING

The principal objective of our analysis of the allocative benefits and costs of the training sponsored by MITCE has been to determine whether the training program as a whole represented an efficient use of society's resources. Table 13 reveals that the training of all MITCE clients in fact added considerably more to aggregate output than it cost. A number of observations are pertinent with respect to this finding.

---

17. See *Cost-Effectiveness Analysis of On-the-Job and Institutional Training Courses*, pp. 7-8 and Appendix A.

18. One important difference between the composition of the indirect cost totals in Table 10 and those cited in *Cost-Effectiveness of On-the-Job and Institutional Training Courses* should be noted. Our totals do not include any allowances for North Carolina Employment Security Commission expenditures in the selection, referral and follow-up of trainees, since these services were performed separately by MITCE and financed under the project's contract with the Department of Labor.

Table 10: "Indirect" Federal and State Weekly Expenditures per MDTA Enrollee in Fiscal Year 1966

Item	Total expenditures in fiscal year 1966 (thousands of dollars)	Expenditures per trainee enrolled (dollars)	
		On-the-job training	Institutional training
U.S. Dept. of Labor, Bureau of Employment Security			
Federal administration	2545	10.8	10.8
N.C. administration	445	82.4	82.4
Costs of processing trainee allowances, N.C.[1]	88		30.3
U.S. Dept. of Labor, Bureau of Apprenticeship and Training[2]			
Federal administration	1305	22.4	
U.S. Dept. of Health, Education and Welfare[1]			
Federal administration	2533		14.3
N.C. administration	84		29.0
Total expenditures per enrollee		115.6	166.8
Expenditures per enrollee/week in fiscal year 1966.		2.2	3.2

1. Applies to institutional training only.

2. Applies to on-the-job training only.

Source: Office of Planning and Policy Development, U.S. Department of Labor.

Table 11: "Indirect" Federal and State Costs per MITCE Trainee

Item	Female on-the-job trainees	Male on-the-job trainees	All institutional trainees	Male institutional trainees
Indirect expenditures per enrollee/week in fiscal year 1966 (dollars)	2.2	2.2	3.2	3.2
Average number of weeks in training	6.0	9.4	22.0	27.1
Total indirect costs per trainee (dollars)	13.2	20.7	70.4	86.7

Sources: Table 10 and text.

Table 12: Total Allocative Costs per MITCE Trainee

Item	Costs per female on-the-job trainee	Costs per male on-the-job trainee	Costs per institutional trainee	Costs per male institutional trainee
MITCE contract costs	1105.9	1105.9	1105.9	1105.9
On-the-job training payments to contractors	68.3	106.8		
Institutional direct course costs			444.9	546.4
Opportunity costs of institutional training			516.4	790.5
Indirect federal and state costs	13.2	20.7	70.4	86.7
Total allocative costs per trainee	1187.4	1233.4	2137.6	2529.5

Sources: Text and Table 11.

Table 13: Allocative Benefit-Cost Ratios per MITCE Trainee

Item	On-the-job training for women	On-the-job training for men	Institutional training for men	Training for all MITCE clients[1]
Present value of allocative benefits	8113	4014	4396	4623
Allocative costs	1187	1233	2530	1503
Allocative benefit-cost ratio	6.8	3.3	1.7	3.1

1. Allocative costs per MITCE trainee were a weighted sum of on-the-job and institutional training costs from Table 12. The weights were the proportions of sample members in each type of training, i.e., 31 per cent of trainee sample members were institutional trainees, 24 per cent were female on-the-job trainees, and 45 per cent were male on-the-job trainees.

Sources: Text and Table 12.

Considering first the benefit side of our calculations, it should be realized that the benefits from training shown in Table 13 are a function of the assumptions made concerning the increases in earnings associated with training in the survey period, the social discount rate, and the annual increase in earnings levels due to economic growth. A variety of assumptions about the magnitude of these variables is employed in Appendix E to derive alternative estimates of the allocative benefits from training. The combination of these assumptions which results in the lowest estimate of the allocative benefits from training fails to upset the conclusion that the training of all MITCE clients added more to aggregate output than it cost.

It should also be recalled that our analysis of the allocative benefits from training has been restricted to measurement of the increases in *earnings* which were associated with training. The likelihood that training courses for MITCE clients were also associated with increases in the nonmarket output of trainees allows one to infer that the allocative benefits from training were somewhat greater than those revealed in Table 13.

It should also be noted that the procedures we have employed in estimating the allocative costs of MITCE lead to a conservative estimate of the allocative efficiency of the training activities of the project. In the first place, transfer payments to on-the-job trainees were treated in our analysis as being "real" costs to society. More importantly, it needs to be stressed again that an objective of MITCE was to experiment with techniques for raising the incomes of a population which was extremely disadvantaged in the labor market. It was not feasible to estimate the costs of the experimental activities of the project, and all such costs were in fact treated as being current costs of training. The training sponsored by MITCE would thus have appeared to be an even more desirable investment for society, had it been possible to estimate actual training costs more accurately.

There were two subsidiary objectives in our analysis of the allocative benefits and costs of the training sponsored by MITCE. In the first place, we wished to compare the allocative benefits and costs of training men as against training women. Our findings in this respect were mixed. On the one hand, it should be recalled that, on average, institutional training was associated with no increases in the earnings levels of women. Consequently, the training of these MITCE clients represented an "inefficient" use of society's resources. On the other hand, the allocative benefit-cost ratio from on-the-job training for women was more than twice as large as the benefit-cost ratio from on-the-job training for men and was four times as large as the benefit-cost ratio from institutional training for men. The inference that on-the-job training for women represented a more efficient use of society's resources does, however, rest on the definition of the allocative benefits from training adopted in this study.[19]

---

19. Appendix E reveals that if the allocative benefits from training had been calculated by the method advocated by Morgan and David, the benefit-cost ratio from on-the-job training for men would have been greater than the benefit-cost ratio from on-the-job training for women.

The Mitce Project

The second supplemental objective of our analysis was to determine which of the two types of skill instruction sponsored by MITCE — on-the-job or institutional training — represented a more efficient use of society's resources. Our results leave no doubt that in allocative terms, on-the-job training was the superior investment for society. With respect to the training of women, the superiority of on-the-job training originated on the side of allocative benefits. With respect to the training of men, the superiority of on-the-job training was attributable to the lower allocative costs of this type of instruction.

THE DISTRIBUTIONAL EFFECTS OF TRAINING

The finding that, by and large, the training activities of MITCE represented an efficient use of society's resources satisfies one of the criteria established above for evaluation of the project. We now have to determine whether the distribution of the earnings increases associated with training was consistent with the objectives of the antipoverty program.

Several standards can be employed in assessing the distributional effects of MITCE's training activities. It was decided in Chapter II that the *sine qua non* of an antipoverty project is that it should raise the incomes of the poor. We should therefore first determine whether the increases in earnings associated with training accrued to people who would otherwise have been poor. If the training sponsored by MITCE satisfies this condition, the next question which naturally arises is whether the earnings increases associated with training proved sufficiently large to shift MITCE clients out of the poverty class. These related issues will now be examined sequentially.

A virtue of the regressions carried out in Chapter III is that we can use them to find the average earnings levels of particular groups of trainees "with" and "without" training. The procedure employed has already been illustrated in finding the opportunity costs to society of institutional training. The regression equations used in finding average weekly earnings levels with and without training were those previously used in constructing Tables 6 and 7. The regression coefficients for all sets other than training status in these equations were simply weighted by the proportion of trainees having the characteristics in question. The resulting weekly earnings figures tell us what trainees would have earned on average in the absence of training, given their geographical location, sex or family status, prior·labor force experience, physical handicaps, education, color, age, mobility and need-achievement status. To find the weekly earnings levels of the various trainee groups with training, we simply add the weekly earnings coefficients associated with training. Finally, to facilitate comparison with poverty indices expressed in terms of yearly incomes, our earnings figures were recomputed on an annual basis.

The two sets of poverty lines which will be used as reference points in comparisons with our estimates of trainee earnings levels are those of Orshansky and Friedman. As noted in Chapter II, the Orshansky poverty lines are used by many executive agencies, and the poverty lines constructed by Friedman are also reasonably well known. Although both of these authors have followed similar general principles in constructing their estimates of poverty level incomes, the poverty lines of Friedman are roughly one-third lower than the equivalent poverty lines of Orshansky. The source of this difference is a matter of some importance in assessments of the relative merits of the poverty levels of the two authors.

The first step taken by both Friedman and Orshansky in the construction of their poverty lines is to estimate the minimum expenditures necessary to provide an adequate diet for families of different sizes. However, both authors acknowledge that no satisfactory generalizations can be made concerning the "adequacy" of nonfood expenditures for households of different compositions. To obtain the income levels which distinguish the poor from the rest of the population, some arbitrary relationship has therefore to be postulated between the budget estimates of minimum-adequacy diets and overall income levels. Orshansky bridges the gap by multiplying the minimum-adequacy food budget by a factor of three; on the grounds that food expenditures make up roughly one-third of the expenditures of the *average* family.[20] Friedman argues that the correct relation between food and nonfood expenditures at the poverty line is what "people who are on the margin of adequate nutrition actually spend for them".[21] Consequently, Friedman multiplies the minimum-adequacy food budget by a factor of 1.67 to derive her poverty levels.

The rationale used by Friedman in constructing her poverty lines appears to be more appropriate than that of Orshansky.[22] Nevertheless, it is of some interest to use the poverty lines of both authors in assessing the distributional effects of the training sponsored by MITCE. In order to do so, we require some additional details concerning the personal circumstances of MITCE clients.

A feature of the poverty income levels of both Friedman and Orshansky is that they vary with the size of the household. For this reason, the relevant poverty levels for male trainees and all MITCE trainees are somewhat higher than those applicable to female MITCE trainees. Male on-the-job trainees and male institutional trainees had an average of four dependents, as did MITCE trainees considered collectively. On the other hand, female on-the-job trainees had an average of three dependents.

---

20. "Counting the Poor", p. 9.

21. Rose D. Friedman, *Poverty: Definition and Perspective* (Washington, D.C.: American Enterprise for Public Policy Research, 1965), p. 35.

22. As Ribich has observed:

since we know nothing about the adequacy of nonfood expenditures, it might be assumed that poor families are more or less rational in their budget allocations and therefore would not allocate 60 per cent of their income on food if that entailed cutbacks on expenditures that were more critical than nutrition.

Education and Poverty, p. 135.

The Mitce Project

The information on the number of dependents of trainees is all that is required to obtain poverty levels for these MITCE clients using Friedman's criteria. However, for families of these sizes, Orshansky's poverty levels also vary with the sex of the head of the household and according to the household's location — whether farm or nonfarm. Orshansky's poverty levels for nonfarm families of different sizes headed by members of either sex were used in our analysis. However, it was felt necessary to make an adjustment to the poverty levels of both Friedman and Orshansky to allow for home production of food by MITCE trainees. Such home production of food constitutes a principal reason for Orshansky's lower poverty levels for farm families.[23] Approximately 35 per cent of MITCE trainees satisfied some of their food requirements by home production, and this group claimed that 23 per cent of their total food requirements were met in this way. Multiplying the two fractions, we find that home production accounted for 8 per cent of the food requirements of all trainees. Accordingly, the minimum-adequacy food budgets appropriate to the various trainee categories were reduced by this amount, and the remainder was multiplied by both Orshansky's multiplier of 3 and Friedman's multiplier of 1.67 to derive poverty levels appropriate to the circumstances of MITCE clients.

Finally, the poverty levels were converted into 1967 prices, in order to reflect economic conditions current in the period when MITCE clients were interviewed. Friedman's poverty levels were originally computed in 1962 prices and Orshansky's poverty levels in 1963 prices. Consequently, Friedman's poverty levels were increased by 9.6 per cent and Orshansky's poverty levels by 8.3 per cent to reflect the increase in the Consumer Price Index by 1967.

The poverty levels of Orshansky and Friedman, adjusted in the manner described above, are compared in Table 14 with our estimates of the average earnings levels of trainees "with" and "without" training.

As can be seen in Table 14, without training the average member of each of the categories of MITCE trainees in which we are interested would have been poor according to the criteria of Orshansky. Moreover, the table also reveals that the earnings increases associated with training were insufficient to push the average earnings levels of members of our training categories over Orshansky's poverty lines. The mean earnings levels of male on-the-job trainees came closest to crossing the poverty threshold, the "poverty income gap" — or dollar amount by which the average incomes of these MITCE clients fell short of the poverty line — being only $216 after training. The average earnings levels for members of each of the other categories of MITCE trainees distinguished in Table 14 were more than twice this dollar amount below Orshansky's poverty lines after training.

The paradox is that using Friedman's criteria as to what constitutes poverty, the average male on-the-job trainee would not have been considered

---

23. See "Counting the Poor", p. 9.

Table 14: Poverty Lines and the Increases in Earnings Associated with Training

Training category	Poverty lines in annual income levels (dollars)		Average annual earnings levels after training (dollars)	
	Following Friedman	Following Orshansky	Without training	With training
Female on-the-job trainees	1800	2341	1101	1857
Male on-the-job trainees	2213	3118	2518	2902
Male institutional trainees	2213	3118	2073	2502
All MITCE trainees[1]	2213	2877	1973	2406

1. The poverty level for all MITCE trainees following Orshansky's criteria was derived by assigning a weight of .69 to her poverty line for a nonfarm family of 4 headed by a male and a weight of .31 to her poverty line for a nonfarm family of 3 headed by a female. These weights reflect the proportions of males and females in our sample.

Sources: "Counting the Poor", p. 28 and *Poverty: Definition and Perspective*, p. 25, adjusted for considerations mentioned in our text.

poor even if he had never been trained. However, without training, the average member of each of the other categories of MITCE trainees distinguished in Table 14 would have been poor by Friedman's standards. Moreover, the earnings increases associated with training did prove sufficient to push the average earnings levels of female on-the-job trainees, male institutional trainees and MITCE trainees considered collectively over Friedman's poverty thresholds.

We may prefer Friedman's poverty lines on the theoretical grounds distinguished earlier and hence judge the training sponsored by MITCE to be an overall success in terms of its distributional effects. However, it is doubtful whether we should rely on any fixed poverty lines or simple "line-crossing" criteria in making such judgements. The procedures of Friedman and Orshansky seem at first sight to be promising approaches to the determination of poverty levels. Nevertheless, these poverty lines lose much of their appeal when the absolute income levels they yield are seen to hinge on the question of whether to multiply minimum-adequacy food budgets by factors of either 1.67 or 3.0. They become even less appealing when doubts are raised about the adequacy of the food budget estimates underlying the calculations.[24]

Dissatisfaction on these grounds with the poverty lines proposed by Orshansky and Friedman — and for that matter other "objective" poverty levels which have been proposed — has led some writers to propose more subjective criteria for use in assessing the distributional effectiveness of antipoverty programs.

These proposals also arise from dissatisfaction with assessments of the effectiveness of antipoverty measures according to whether they raise the incomes of antipoverty program clients above poverty lines, or according to whether they reduce the poverty income gap. The deficiencies of both of these criteria for assessing the effectiveness of antipoverty programs can be illustrated with reference to the findings from our evaluation of the MITCE project.

Both the goal of raising the incomes of antipoverty program clients above poverty income levels and the goal of closing the poverty income gap imply that once the incomes of antipoverty program clients rise above the poverty level, no value should be attached to any further increases in their incomes. Thus, if we were employing Friedman's poverty thresholds as reference points in our evaluation of MITCE, we would disregard the average improvement in earnings levels associated with on-the-job training for men. Yet by most standards, the alternative earnings levels of these MITCE clients without training were still very low, and the increase in average earnings levels associated with training represented a significant improvement in the circumstances of the individuals concerned. Our criteria for assessing the effectiveness of antipoverty programs should reflect the fact that we are not indifferent to such income gains above the poverty line.

---

24. On this point, see Ribich, *Education and Poverty*, p. 135.

A second deficiency of the "line-crossing" and "gap-reducing" criteria of the effectiveness of antipoverty programs arises in their treatment of income gains which fall short of the poverty line. Thus, MITCE would be considered worthless as an antipoverty measure if our criterion of the program's effectiveness was whether it succeeded in raising the incomes of its clients above the Orshansky poverty lines. MITCE would be considered more worthwhile if our criterion of the project's effectiveness was whether it succeeded in closing the poverty income gap below Orshansky's poverty lines, but this criterion assigns the same weight to equal increases in the incomes of individuals below the poverty levels. Using this criterion, we would regard the roughly $400 improvement in the average earnings levels of both male institutional trainees and male on-the-job trainees as being of equal importance. Yet the increases in the average earnings levels of the male institutional trainees should mean more to us on any rational grounds, since these individuals would have had lower average earnings levels without training. Our criteria for assessing the effectiveness of antipoverty programs should reflect this concern.

The most elegant solution to these problems of which the writer is aware has been put forward by Ribich. Treating the reduction of poverty as an externality to the average citizen, he suggests that it be dealt with as a special case of the theory of public goods. He proposes that two poverty lines be established. Increases in incomes accruing to people below the upper line "would provide our representative individual a positive external benefit for which he would exchange some amount of money".[25] Above this line, Ribich hypothesizes that the same representative individual would feel "no particular social obligation to a fellow citizen and would not be inclined to make any meaningful sacrifice to see him rise still higher".[26] The lower poverty line is "the income level which, at the going cost of antipoverty programs, our representative citizen is indifferent about altering upwards".[27]

Ribich's criteria for evaluating antipoverty projects derive added attractiveness from the fact that they allow us to integrate assessments of the distributional and allocative effects of such projects. Thus, Ribich would weight the allocative benefit-cost ratios for antipoverty projects according to the income ranges of the people affected by these programs. The weight would approach zero at his upper poverty line and would increase the further income levels were below this line.[28] This weighting system reflects the assumption that a representative citizen would value more highly a dollar's worth of relief to those people at the severest levels of poverty than a dollar's worth of relief to those who, while still poor, are at slightly higher income levels.

---

25. *Ibid.*, p. 26.

26. *Ibid.*

27. *Ibid.*, p. 27.

28. *Ibid.*, pp. 29-30

The Mitce Project

The practical problems in applying Ribich's standards are obviously those of arriving at a public consensus as to the two poverty lines and the weighting system which should be used in assessing income increases associated with antipoverty programs. Lacking such information, we can only indicate roughly how the application of these criteria might affect our judgements on the MITCE project.

The comparison between the types of training sponsored by MITCE is not difficult. As was seen in Table 13, the highest allocative benefit-cost ratio for any of our categories of training was that associated with on-the-job training for women. Moreover, it was also estimated above that if training had never taken place, the average earnings of these female MITCE clients would have been lower than the average earnings of individuals in other MITCE training categories for which benefit-cost ratios were calculated. Thus, a comparison in which the allocative benefit-cost ratios for the various training categories were weighted by the alternative earnings levels of trainees would clearly reflect most favourably on on-the-job training for women.

Regarding the comparison between on-the-job and institutional training for men, we have seen that an unweighted comparison of benefit-cost ratios is unfavourable to institutional training. A weighted comparison of benefit-cost ratios would be less adverse to institutional training, but would be unlikely to reverse judgements reached solely on the basis of the unweighted benefit-cost ratios. Without training, the average annual earnings of male institutional trainees would have been $445 lower than the average annual earnings of male on-the-job trainees. However, it seems doubtful that we would wish to value this difference by weighting the benefit-cost ratio for institutional training as much as 87 per cent greater than that for on-the-job training. Yet the relative weight attached to institutional training for men would have to be this much greater than that for on-the-job training for men, simply to offset the difference in the unweighted benefit-cost ratios.

The benefit-cost ratios for the MITCE project as a whole would also benefit from a weighted comparison with those of other antipoverty programs. While we do not know what poverty levels might be determined by public consensus, we can observe that few if any published benefit-cost analyses of antipoverty programs have dealt with populations having as low average earnings levels as those of MITCE clients. Indeed, it is pertinent to remark that few antipoverty measures have been shown to have allocative benefit-cost ratios as large as that found for the MITCE project. This is one of the matters that will be considered in our final chapter when we bring together the findings of our study.

CHAPTER V

CONCLUSIONS

The objective of our analysis has been to infer what effects antipoverty training programs of the kind authorized under the Manpower Development and Training Act have on the incomes of trainees and on national output. Results from past benefit-cost analyses of MDTA-type programs have often been cited as indicating that these programs both increase the incomes of the poor and add more to national output than they cost. The conclusion reached in the present study is that these inferences from past analyses are unwarranted.

In the first place, we have contended that the training programs studied in past benefit-cost analyses did not deal with a population of primary concern to the antipoverty program. The training studied took place in a period before MDTA was redirected to training those considered to be disadvantaged in the labor market, and before similar training programs directed to the poor were created by additional federal legislation. The relevance of the results from past benefit-cost analyses of MDTA-type training is clearly limited by these changes in the emphasis of federal training programs.

We have also argued that insufficiently stringent criteria were used to measure the benefits and costs of the training studied in previous analyses. It is our contention that the productivity of workers should be measured in their hourly wage rates, and that increases in earnings levels associated with training programs which are solely attributable to increases in the employment of trainees may simply represent transfers of income from nontrainees to trainees. Because employers may use educational levels or skill qualifications as screening devices in slack labor markets, the better educated and even those workers having training program diplomas may be considered employable at the expense of their less educated or less qualified counterparts. Consequently, earnings differentials in slack labor markets may exaggerate productivity differentials among workers having different educational or skill levels. We have also noted that officials in charge of MDTA-type training programs are often required to search for employment for those trainees who complete their courses of instruction. These official job-placement activities could make a substantial difference to the employment prospects of trainees when labor markets are slack. The effects of such employer and official discrimination in favor of train-

Conclusions

ing program completors should not, of course, be confused with any increases in the productivity of workers which may be associated with training programs.

So far as could be ascertained, past benefit-cost analyses of MDTA-type training programs do not indicate that the training studied was associated with increases in the hourly wage rates of workers. The increases in the earnings of workers shown to be associated with training in these analyses appear to have been entirely attributable to increases in the employment of trainees. It should be noted that the training studied in these analyses took place in slack labor markets. Data are also available which support the hypothesis that the increases in the employment of trainees reported in these past analyses were attributable to the job-placement activities of training program officials. We therefore concluded that there was no evidence that the training studied in former analyses raised the productivity of trainees, and that the increases in the incomes of trainees reported in these analyses may have been achieved at the expense of less fortunate members of the labor force, such as those who were excluded from training programs by the selection criteria adopted in these programs.

The benefit-cost analysis undertaken in the present study dealt with an MDTA training project in which the average trainee suffered from greater disadvantages in the labor market than the average MDTA trainee, and had "expected" earnings well below the poverty income lines adopted by many executive agencies. Our analysis revealed that the training sponsored by Manpower Improvement through Community Effort, considered as a whole, was associated with substantial increases in the earnings of the project's clients, and also in their productivity as measured in their hourly wage rates. We concluded that the training sponsored by MITCE satisfied the distributional objective of the antipoverty program, and added more to national output than it cost.

Other objectives in our evaluation of MITCE were to compare the allocative and distributional effects of training for men and women, and of institutional and on-the-job training. Our analysis revealed that the allocative benefit-cost ratio from on-the-job training for women was much greater than the respective allocative benefit-cost ratios from either on-the-job training for men or institutional training for men. Moreover, without training, the average earnings levels of women who were on-the-job trainees would have been much lower than the average earnings levels of male MITCE clients. Thus, not only did on-the-job training for women appear to represent a more "efficient" use of society's resources than training for men, but it was also the most desirable form of training from the point of view of the distributional objective of the antipoverty program.

Not all of the training for women sponsored by MITCE can, however, be considered satisfactory in terms of its distributional and allocative effects. Thus, institutional training was not associated with increases in the average earnings levels of female MITCE clients. It is necessary to note that this institutional training may have increased the nonmarket incomes of female MITCE clients.

Equally, however, training for other MITCE clients may have had similar benefits which we also could not measure.

The obvious implication from our evaluation of the MITCE project is that on-the-job training should receive greater emphasis than institutional training as an antipoverty measure. Our analysis left little doubt that the on-the-job training sponsored by MITCE represented a more efficient use of society's resources than the institutional training sponsored by the project. Where rough comparisons could be made between the earnings differentials associated with training for particular occupations, it appeared that institutional training was the superior form of instruction. However, some poor choices were made in the selection of institutional training occupations. This factor, together with the lack of motivation of female institutional trainees to use their training in employment, was thought to account for the apparent failure of institutional training to raise the average earnings levels of women. Indeed, the findings from our analysis of institutional training for women lead to two immediate policy implications. In the first place, it is recommended that the United States Department of Labor should pay closer attention to the choices of training occupations made by MDTA project officials in the field. In particular, the case for the provision of training in "skill-shortage" occupations should be re-examined. Secondly, if the objective of training women is to raise their earnings levels, it appears that on-the-job training has a natural advantage over institutional training. The present study demonstrates that one can be more certain that a woman who undertakes on-the-job training is committed to the labor force than a woman who undertakes institutional training.

Our analysis also indicated that the costs of the institutional training sponsored by MITCE were greater than those of on-the-job training sponsored by the project. The fact that the benefit-cost ratio from on-the-job training for men was greater than that from institutional training for men can be ascribed to the differences in the costs of the two types of instruction. Institutional training was actually associated with larger increases in the average earnings levels of men than on-the-job training. However, the difference in the costs of the two types of instruction proved to be sufficient to outweigh the difference in the benefits from the two types of training.

From a distributional point of view, on-the-job training was also found to have greater merits than institutional training. Thus, in general, on-the-job training was found to be associated with larger increases in the average earnings levels of MITCE clients who had characteristics considered to convey disadvantages in the labor market.

Another objective of our analysis was to infer whether training served to offset specific characteristics of MITCE clients considered to entail disadvantages in the labor market. Our analysis revealed that training was, in most cases, associated with larger increases in the earnings of MITCE clients considered to be disadvantaged in the labor market, than for the MITCE clientele as a whole. The only disadvantaged group for which no increase in earnings was associated with any type of training was that of persons under 21 years of age. No explanation could be found for this result, which is discouraging in view of the importance attached to training this age-group in the national MDTA program. It could be that programs such as the Job Corps, which train young people away from their home environment, represent more suitable means of raising the earnings levels of youths in the poverty population. This problem clearly warrants further attention.

From the point of view of the policy implications of our evaluation of MITCE, it is necessary to consider our findings in the wider context of the antipoverty program as a whole. Specific questions that need to be answered are whether the results of the MITCE project could be duplicated in similar projects, and how the findings from our evaluation compare with the findings from evaluations of other antipoverty measures.

The writer sees no reason to believe that the results achieved in the MITCE project could not be duplicated in other programs having a similarly disadvantaged clientele. In fact, there is every reason to believe that expanded training projects for the disadvantaged would have greater benefit-cost ratios than those found for the MITCE project. It should be recalled that MITCE was an MDTA Experimental and Demonstration Project, with the objective of seeing how training could best be used to aid a population which was severely disadvantaged in the labor market. In regular MDTA training programs for the disadvantaged which did not have these experimental objectives, one would naturally expect costs to be considerably pared.

Of course, it needs to be stressed that training programs for the poor involve greater costs than training programs for a clientele which is not disadvantaged in the labor market. Higher costs for training the poor follow inescapably from the fact that expenditures on items such as counselling services are necessary to make this training effective. The MITCE project demonstrates that training programs for the rural poor are even more costly than training programs for the urban poor. The higher costs of training for the rural poor are an inevitable result of the greater geographic dispersion of trainees and the problems of communication posed by inadequate and costly transportation facilities.

We also need to observe that our findings relate to a training project which only marginally affected the labor markets in which it operated. It might be thought that expanded training programs, based on the MITCE model, which have a larger impact on labor markets, would also tend to have reduced benefits and higher marginal costs. However, the findings from studies of the returns from education do not suggest that such declines in the returns from expanded training programs are inevitable. Rates of return to education in the United States do not appear to have declined over time, despite a massive upgrading in the educational levels of the labor force over the period for which rates of return have been calculated. Hypotheses advanced to explain this phenomenon would also lead one to believe that the rates of return from vocational training might not decrease with an expansion in the latter form of skill acquisition.[1]

The emphasis that training should receive in total antipoverty expenditures depends, of course, partly on the findings from assessments of the distributional and allocative effects of alternative antipoverty measures. To the writer's knowledge, birth control is the only antipoverty measure which is reputed to have greater distributional and allocative effects than the training analyzed in the present study.[2] Accordingly, it is reasonable to conclude that expenditures on training should constitute a substantial proportion of expenditures in the antipoverty program. It also needs to be added, however, that little is known (or has been published) about the effects of many possible antipoverty measures. For instance, the writer feels that information on the effects of harnessing training programs for the southern rural poor to relocation of trainees in areas where economic opportunities are greater would be valuable. Information on the effects of such antipoverty measures in southern contexts is particularly necessary. As Henry Simons has reminded us, "The great American problem of poverty and underprivilege concerns Southern Labor."[3]

---

1.   For instance, a possible reason for the failure of rates of return from education to decline over time is the finding of several writers that there may be high elasticities of substitution among workers with different educational levels. See Samuel Bowles, *Planning Educational Systems,* pp. 43-49, and "Aggregation of Labor Inputs in the Economics of Growth and Planning: Experiments with a Two-Level CES Function", *Journal of Political Economy* 78 (February, 1970): 69; Marcelo Selowsky, "On the Measurement of Education's Contribution to Growth", *Quarterly Journal of Economics* 83 (August, 1969): 462; and Finis Welch, "Education in Production", *Journal of Political Economy* 78 (February, 1970): 51-53. Bowles hypothesizes that such high elasticities of substitution may be partly ascribable to the fact that on-the-job training is a good substitute for education in production. See *Planning Educational Systems,* p. 61. Of course, this hypothesis might also lead one to believe that the rate of return from on-the-job training would stay fairly constant with changes in the levels of the on-the-job training of the labor force.

2.   This assumption rests largely on hearsay and inference. For instance, according to *The Daily Manpower Reporter* of 18 July, 1966, citing an article in *The Christian Science Monitor* on 12 July, 1966:

> The federal government is also recruiting operations research in its 'war on poverty'. For example, one study found that family planning would be a highly 'cost-effective' program to reduce poverty. If it had been launched a generation ago, there would be about 4.5 million fewer poor people in the country today.

Published analyses of the benefits and costs of birth control measures in underdeveloped countries allow us to infer more strongly, however, that these programs would have the effects noted in the text. See for instance Stephen Enke, "The Economic Aspects of Slowing Population Growth", *The Economic Journal* 76 (March, 1966): 44-56.

3.   *Economic Policy for a Free Society* (Chicago: University of Chicago Press, 1948), p. 135, cited by Marshall R. Colberg, *Human Capital in Southern Development, 1939-1963* (Chapel Hill, N.C.: The University of North Carolina Press, 1965), p. 3.

APPENDIX A

SAMPLING PROCEDURE AND RESPONSE VARIATION IN THE SURVEY OF MITCE CLIENTS

Sampling Procedure

As was noted in Chapter I, MITCE personnel completed standard client-description forms for all MITCE clients who were considered eligible and available for training — whether these individuals were subsequently trained or not.[1] These forms provided some prior knowledge of the characteristics of trainees and nontrainees which was used in the construction of a stratified sample for the survey of MITCE clients. However, the population sampled did not consist of all MITCE clients who were eligible and available for training during the period covered by the first contract of MITCE with the U.S. Department of Labor. Only those trainees who had completed their courses of instruction at least a year before interviewing for the survey commenced were included in the population. It was considered that other MITCE trainees would not have had representative earnings and employment records in the after-training period. This restriction primarily affected institutional trainees, roughly one-half of whom were excluded from the population on this ground.

Choices had to be made in selecting the criteria according to which the sample was stratified, and the decision to sample on the basis of age, sex and training status meant that other possible stratifications — e.g. on race — were sacrificed. The sample rate for each age, sex and training status category was influenced primarily by the overall research objectives of the project and by findings in the earlier analysis of the client-description forms, particularly regarding cell size. For example, two principal objectives of the project were to estimate the effects on earnings associated with institutional and on-the-job training, and of training men as against women. However, the number of female and institutional trainees in the population was small, and so these groups were sampled in their entirety. The sample rates for these and other sample categories are set out in Table A1.

Response Variation in the Survey

Because of the implications for the statistical analysis of survey data, it is important to determine whether there were significant differences in response rates of MITCE clients in the various sex, age and training status categories of our sample. In Table A1 the number and proportions of MITCE clients interviewed are given for each sampling category and for summary classifications of training status. A chi-square test on the data in Table A1 allows us to accept

---

1. This client-description form was U.S. Department of Labor MDTA training form No. MT. 101.

Appendix A

Table A1: Sample and Response Rates for the Survey of MITCE Clients

Characteristic	Number in universe	Number in sample	Number of respondents	Sample rate (per cent)	Response rate (per cent)
Male on-the-job trainees, under 21 years of age*	69	43	29	62	67
Male on-the-job trainees, 21-33 years of age	163	52	33	32	63
Male on-the-job trainees, 34-43 years of age	70	45	35	64	78
Male on-the-job trainees, 44 years and over	43	31	23	72	72
Female on-the-job trainees, all age groups	75	75	63	100	84
Male institutional trainees, all age groups	89	89	61	100	67
Female institutional trainees, all age groups	25	25	20	100	80
Total trainees	534	360	264	67	73
Male nontrainees, under 21 years of age	62	25	16	40	64
Male nontrainees, 21-33 years of age	135	40	27	30	68
Male nontrainees, 34-43 years of age	78	31	21	40	68
Male nontrainees, 44 years and over	109	33	23	30	70
Male nontrainees, age unknown	68	20	15	29	75
Female nontrainees, under 21 years of age	34	19	11	56	58
Female nontrainees, 21-33 years of age	89	26	18	29	69
Female nontrainees, 34-43 years of age	71	25	22	35	85
Female nontrainees, 44 years and over	62	21	17	34	81
Female nontrainees, age unknown	30	10	10	33	100
Total nontrainees	738	250	180	34	72

*Age was calculated as of 1 January, 1966.

the hypothesis that there was no difference between the response rates of *all* trainees and *all* nontrainees at the .01 level of significance. However, it is evident from Table A1 that more women were interviewed than men, and a chi-square test confirmed that the difference in response rates between the sexes was significant at the .01 level. It also appeared that older MITCE clients were more likely to be interviewed than younger MITCE clients. When respondents and those nonrespondents whose ages were known were classified according to broad age-groupings,[2] a chi-square test indicated that the differences in response rates by age were significant at the .01 level.

Weighting of Survey Observations

The principal objective of the statistical analysis undertaken in this study has been to obtain unbiased estimates of the effects on earnings and employment associated with the training of MITCE clients. Biased estimates of these effects would have resulted from the use of unweighted survey data in the analysis. Because sampling rates and response rates differed by age, sex and training status, some members of the MITCE client population were more likely to be interviewed than others. To correct for this factor in the regression analysis of Chapter III, each interview was weighted by the reciprocal of the product of the sample and response rates for the sample category in which the interview occurred.[3] Thus the regression coefficients in Chapter III are not biased because our sample members had varying probabilities of being interviewed.

---

2.   That is, under 21 years, 21-33 years, 34-43 years, and over 44 years of age as of 1 January, 1966.

3.   This method of eliminating sample bias arising where sample units are selected with known but varying probabilities is outlined by Morris H. Hansen, William N. Hurwitz, and William G. Madow, *Sample Survey Methods and Theory* (New York: John Wiley and Sons, 1964), p. 61. An example of the use of this method which is nearly identical to our own is given in Morgan *et al., Income and Welfare in the United States,* p. 451.

APPENDIX B

ASPECTS OF THE MEASUREMENT OF LABOR EARNINGS OF MITCE CLIENTS

The Labor Earnings of the Self-Employed

As might have been expected, most of the self-employed respondents encountered in our survey of MITCE clients were tenant farmers. These respondents were asked to provide annual data on gross farm income, farm operating expenses, the value of any land, buildings or equipment owned by themselves and the number of hours worked on the farm by themselves or unpaid family members. Interviewing for the survey of MITCE clients was conducted late in the crop year of 1967, when many farmers had not completed the sale of their products. The 1967 gross farm income of these respondents was therefore an estimate provided by themselves.

To obtain the labor earnings of the tenant farmer, farm operating expenses and 6% of the estimated value of the respondent's investment in the farm were first subtracted from gross farm income.[1] Hours worked on the farm by the respondent and unpaid family members were next accumulated to obtain farm labor hours, an hour's work by an unpaid family member under 14 years of age being valued as half an hour's work by an adult. Farm income net of expenses and the return to capital was then divided by farm labor hours, and the quotient multiplied by the hours worked by the respondent to obtain his return from labor on the farm.

Adjustments of a similar nature were made to find the labor earnings of the few self-employed survey respondents who were not tenant farmers.

Wage Supplements

Although data were collected on a wide range of fringe benefits and costs associated with employment in our survey of MITCE clients, there are problems in incorporating these data into measures of labor earnings. Some of these problems involve difficulties of measurement; others are of the philosophical

---

1. The assumption of a 6% rate of return to farm capital was made following the work of Morgan and David, who employed this assumption in their own estimates of the returns to investment in education. See "Education and Income", p. 426.

kind which have plagued national income statisticians for years. Brief illustrations of both kinds of problems will be given, together with an outline of the treatment of these problems in the present study.

There was little difficulty in incorporating employer payroll expenditures such as bonuses, paid vacation and paid sick leave into the aggregate earnings of MITCE clients. The provision of work clothing by employers, housing (a fringe benefit often received by tenant farmers), and meals (a fringe benefit often received by domestic servants), although not payroll expenditures, were also incorporated into aggregate earnings. The values attributed to the last three items were, of course, imputations provided directly by the respondent.

While other fringe benefits may in principle be quantifiable, there may be difficulties in collecting data on them where, as in the present study, a survey is restricted to recipients of the benefits. The respondent may simply be unaware of the savings to himself in certain wage and salary supplements; we found this to be general in the cases of life insurance, hospitalization, and retirement plans sponsored by employers. Such costs to employers could be measured at the source, as has been done by the Department of Labor.[2] Such a solution was, however, out of the question in a study of the present type.

Following the work of Carroll and Ihnen, data were also collected on a number of possible costs associated with either obtaining or continuing in particular forms of employment, such as fees to employment agencies and the costs of tools and work clothing required by the employer.[3] However, such items were not taken into account in our measures of labor earnings. It was decided that these costs could not be unequivocally regarded as conditions of employment involving expenditures which would otherwise not have been made by the worker.

The fringe benefits that were measured in our survey of MITCE clients proved to be comparatively unimportant as a component of average weekly earnings. The mean after-training earnings of trainees were raised from $44.0 per week (the standard deviation being $25.3) to $45.4 per week (the standard deviation being $26.0) by the inclusion of fringe benefits. Correspondingly, the mean after-training earnings of nontrainees were raised from $30.8 per week (the standard deviation being $24.7) to $32.4 per week (the standard deviation being $25.5). Given the standard deviations, the mean weekly earnings of neither trainees nor nontrainees were significantly affected by the inclusion of fringe benefits.

---

2.   See for instance, Arnold Strasser, "The Changing Structure of Employment Compensation", *Monthly Labor Review* 89 (Sept., 1966): 955.

3.   Adger B. Carroll and Loren A. Ihnen, "Costs and Returns for Two Years of Postsecondary Schooling: A Pilot Study", *Journal of Political Economy* 75 (Dec., 1967): 873.

APPENDIX C

THE MOTIVATION VARIABLES

Post-war years have witnessed some important applications of psychological and sociological theory in the explanation of economic phenomena. The motivational variables employed in our analysis are a product of this research.

According to psychological theory, people have personality dispositions or motives which are reasonably stable over time. In recent research, these motives have been classified under three main headings: the "needs" for achievement, affiliation and power. The motive which is most relevant to explanations of economic behavior is the need for achievement. According to James N. Morgan,

> A person with a strong motive to achieve tends to derive satisfaction from overcoming obstacles by his own efforts. He takes calculated risks, rather than playing long shots or being overly cautious ... the need for achievement seems most likely to be associated with upward mobility, long hours of work, desires to accumulate capital and educate one's children, and entrepreneurial activity. [1]

Perhaps the most widely known application of the theory of need-achievement in economic enquiry is also the most wide-ranging in its findings. According to David S. McLelland "n[eed] achievement is a key factor in the rise and fall of the economic base of civilizations". [2] In less far-reaching enquiries, James N. Morgan and his colleagues at the Survey Research Center (S.R.C.) of the University of Michigan have found that indices of the need-achievement motive contribute to the statistical explanation of such variables as hourly earnings, income from savings, and years of education completed by the children of respondents in S.R.C. surveys. [3] In fact, the researchers at the University of Michigan have pioneered in adapting tests of the need-achievement motive for use in cross-section surveys. Since the S.R.C. tests were adopted for use in our MITCE survey questionnaire, a brief account will be given of the methodology used in constructing these tests.

---

1.   "The Achievement Motive and Economic Behavior", *Economic Development and Cultural Change* 12 (April, 1964): 244.

2.   *The Achieving Society* (Princeton, N.J.: Van Nostrand, 1961), p. 157.

3.   Morgan, "Achievement Motive and Economic Behavior", p. 263.

The Theory Underlying the S.R.C. Motivation Tests

Since research supported the hypothesis that the need-achievement motive could be measured by quantifying the degree to which people rated highly success in the high prestige occupations with substantial barriers to entry and rated lowly success in low prestige jobs, Morgan and his colleagues asked respondents the following question:

We are interested in how people compare occupations. How do you think most people would feel if a boy of theirs chose each of these types of work?[4]

The respondents were confronted sequentially with nine occupations for which "prestige" rankings had previously been established in a national survey, and were given a choice among the responses of "not happy", "wouldn't mind", "happy", "very happy" and "delighted". These responses were scaled in value from one to five (in the order given) and the resulting scores were regressed against the national survey "prestige" scores of the occupations, the latter being ranked from one to nine. The slope of the resulting regression line was taken as the individual's need-achievement index.

An important link between achievement motivation and behavior is one's belief concerning whether undertaking a particular course of action will lead to the expected outcome. The Michigan researchers measured this belief by the question,

Some people say that people get ahead by their own hard work; others say that lucky breaks or help from other people are more important. What do you think?[5]

Results from this test were combined with the need-achievement index to form a combined "motive-expectancy" variable in much of the analysis done by Morgan and his colleagues.

The theory was that those who had a high need for achievement, and believed that hard work would result in success would work the hardest.[6]

Use of the Motivation Variables in our Analysis

The questions to determine the need-achievement motive and the joint motivation-expectancy index were adopted verbatim from S.R.C. questionnaires for use in our survey. However the technique employed in the calculation of the need-achievement index was slightly altered in our study. Morgan and his colleagues regressed the occupation evaluation score of the respondent against a "prestige" ranking of occupations derived from a 1950 survey of the National Opinion Research Center. This 1950 ranking was comparatively ancient when

---

4.   *Ibid.*, p. 247.

5.   *Ibid.*, p. 257.

6.   *Ibid.*, p. 257.

Appendix C

Morgan and his colleagues carried out their initial tests of the need-achievement motive, in a 1959 S.R.C. survey. Since prestige rankings of occupations change over time, Morgan has suggested that a better index of prestige would be provided by using the rankings developed in the actual 1959 S.R.C. survey.[7] This suggestion was followed in our own analysis, and the resulting variable will henceforth be described as *need-achievement index A*.

However, an eight year interval elapsed between the 1959 S.R.C. analysis and our own survey, and changes in the prestige ranking of occupations are just as likely to have occurred in this period. Table C1 does indeed reveal some interesting differences between prestige rankings of occupations in the two surveys.

Some of the differences in the prestige ranking of occupations between the two studies could, of course, also be due to regional and cultural bias; the 1959 S.R.C. survey was national in scope, while our MITCE survey was restricted to a predominantly nonwhite Southern rural population. For this reason, it was felt that there would be some advantage in using an alternative need-achievement index derived by regressing respondent evaluation scores against the overall occupational prestige ranking established in our survey of MITCE. The variable constructed in this way will henceforth be referred to as *need-achievement index B*.

Results from Tests of the Motivation Variables

Table C2 indicates the net change in average weekly earnings of MITCE clients associated with the various need-achievement and attitude to hard work/need-achievement sets. It should be noted that the regression equations used in constructing Table C2 contained all of the independent variable sets used in constructing Table 5 of the text; only the need-achievement set being altered as specified above. Thus Table C2 indicates the changes in average weekly earnings associated with the several motivation variables when the effects of geographical location, prior labor force experience, physical handicaps, color, age, mobility, education, family status and training status are held constant. As can be seen from Table C2, need-achievement index A was the only motivation set which had at least one significant regression coefficient. On this basis, it was selected for inclusion in the regressions of the text.

---

7.   *Ibid.,* p. 250.

Table C1: Mean Occupation Evaluation Scores and "Prestige" Rankings of Occupations from a 1959 National Sample Undertaken by the Survey Research Center, and from the 1967 Benefit-Cost Survey of MITCE

Occupation	Mean occupation evaluation score: S.R.C. study	Occupation "prestige" ranking: S.R.C. study	Mean occupation evaluation score: MITCE study	Occupation "prestige" ranking: MITCE study
Night-watchman	1.25	1	1.56	1
Bus driver	1.75	2	2.29	2
Mail carrier	2.15	3	2.71	5
Carpenter	2.30	4	2.40	3
Auto mechanic	2.31	5	2.61	4
Bookkeeper	2.54	6	2.99	6
Highschool teacher	3.19	7	3.47	7
Drugstore owner	3.33	8	3.84	9
Doctor	3.96	9	3.69	8

Sources: Morgan, "Achievement Motive and Economic Behavior", p. 247, and the MITCE survey.

Appendix C

Table C2: Multiple Regressions of Weekly Earnings after Training on Respondent Characteristics:

Respondents Classified by Alternative Measures of Motivation[1]

	Weekly earnings (dollars)	
	Net regression coefficient	Standard error of the regression coefficient
Variable 1.		
Need-achievement index A:		
Lowest third of scores	- 2.97*	1.41
Medium third of scores[2]	0	0
Highest third of scores	-1.29	1.44
Regression constant	38.39**	2.96
Variable 2.		
Need-achievement index B:		
Lowest third of scores	-1.02	1.43
Medium third of scores[2]	0	0
Highest third of scores	0.28	1.44
Regression constant	39.76**	2.84
Variable 3.		
Hard work is equal to or more important than luck; need-achievement index A is in:		
Lowest third of scores[2]	0	0
Medium third of scores	2.44	1.68
Highest third of scores	0.63	1.74
Hard work is less important than luck; need-achievement index A is in:		
Lowest third of scores	- 0.69	2.37
Medium third of scores	- 0.71	2.55
Highest third of scores	1.80	2.49
Attitude to hard work or need-achievement n.a.	1.24	2.55
Regression constant	38.39**	2.99

Table C2: continued.

	Weekly earnings (dollars)	
	Net regression coefficient	Standard error of the regression coefficient
Variable 4.		
Hard work is equal to or more important than luck, need-achievement index B is in:		
Lowest third of scores[2]	0	0
Medium third of scores	0.20	1.72
Highest third of scores	0.74	1.70
Hard work is less important than luck, need-achievement index B is in:		
Lowest third of scores	-1.12	2.39
Medium third of scores	-1.07	2.59
Highest third of scores	0.19	2.43
Attitude to hard work or need-achievement n.a.	0.40	2.54
Regression constant	39.48**	3.01

n.a. not available.

* Significant at the .05 level.

** Significant at the .01 level.

1. 444 observations.

2. The element of the set which enters the constant term.

For all 4 regression equations containing the different need-achievement variables, the coefficient of determination, adjusted for degrees of freedom, was 0.49. The standard errors of estimated weekly earnings for the four equations were: Variable 1, $19.36; Variable 2, $19.40; Variable 3, $19.44; and Variable 4, $19.47.

APPENDIX D

THE INFLUENCE OF DISTANCE TO TRAINING AND THE TIME PERIOD IN WHICH TRAINING TOOK PLACE ON THE EARNINGS OF TRAINEES

Great interest was attached in Chapter I to ascertaining the influence of two variables on MITCE's success in increasing the earnings of its clients by training. Both variables may have influenced the dropout rate from training, and as was established in Chapter III, dropouts from training had significantly lower net average weekly earnings than MITCE clients who completed their training.

The first factor considered was the daily distance the client had to travel to training. One would expect that the greater the distance, the more likely it would be that a client might not complete his training.

The *MITCE Final Report* also asserted that a second factor affecting completion rates was the amount of counselling the trainee received. There is evidence that when such counselling services were increased, the number of dropouts from training was reduced.[1] This discovery — and the necessary remedial action to solve the problem — took place at the end of the first contract of MITCE, and so its effects on the respondents we studied would be marginal. The time period in which a client received his training *during* the first MITCE contract could nevertheless be important; it is conceivable that as the MITCE personnel gained experience, the effectiveness of training would also have improved.

Both hypotheses were tested in simple forms. Following an inspection of the distribution of daily round-trip miles to training sites, the sample was partitioned into three roughly equal parts: trainees having to travel less than 16 miles, 16-30 miles, and over 30 miles respectively. To test the time-period hypothesis, the trainees were classified according to whether they finished training in 1965 or 1966. The actual test of these hypotheses was to see whether — in a regression for trainees only — the dummy variables representing the time period of training and the distance travelled to training were associated with significant net increases in average weekly earnings after training. Other independent variables in the regression equation allowed for the effects of

---

1. *MITCE Final Report,* p. 50.

location, prior labor force experience, physical handicaps, race, age, mobility, education, need-achievement status, family status and the occupation for which the respondent was trained.

Table D1 shows that net of the influence of other independent variables, neither the distance to training nor the year in which the respondent was trained was associated with significant net increases in average weekly earnings after training. These findings should nevertheless be qualified by a consideration of other factors. In the first place, as was seen in Chapter I, rural trainees can incur substantial personal costs in travelling to training, and we should not be indifferent to these costs. Secondly, MITCE's discovery that trainee completion rates could be influenced by varying the amount of counselling services is clearly important. The impact of this discovery would have been felt in MITCE's second contract; our data did not provide a fair test of its effects.

Table D1: Multiple Regressions of Weekly Earnings after Training on Trainee Characteristics:

Trainees Classified by Distance Travelled to Training and by Time Period of Training[1]

	Weekly earnings (dollars)	
	Net regression coefficient	Standard error of the net regression coefficient
Daily miles to training		
01-15 miles	- 0.3	2.5
16-30 miles[2]	0	0
31 miles and over	1.2	2.6
Year ended training		
1966[2]	0	0
1965	- 0.5	3.0
Regression constant	50.6**	5.0

** Significant at the .01 level.

1. 262 observations.

2. The element of the set which enters the constant term.

The coefficient of determination for the equation, adjusted for degrees of freedom was 0.37, and the standard error of estimated weekly earnings for the equation was $20.2.

APPENDIX E

ALTERNATIVE ESTIMATES OF THE ALLOCATIVE BENEFITS AND BENEFIT-COST RATIOS FROM THE TRAINING SPONSORED BY MITCE

The estimates in Chapter IV of the total allocative benefits from training MITCE clients were influenced by the assumptions made concerning the allocative benefits from training in the survey period, the social discount rate used in converting future earnings streams to "present values", and the estimated increase in future earnings levels due to economic growth. It was noted that some researchers would have employed rather different assumptions in estimating the allocative benefits from training in the survey period. It was also pointed out that there is considerable divergence of opinion on the magnitude of the social discount rate that should be used in benefit-cost analyses of public expenditure programs. Moreover, substantial uncertainty is inherent in estimates of the future increment in earnings levels arising from productivity growth in the economy. In the circumstances, it is an appropriate task in this appendix to derive alternative estimates of the total allocative benefits from training using a variety of values for the variables listed above. The estimates of total allocative training benefits emerging from this "sensitivity" analysis will also be compared with the allocative costs of training, in order to determine whether we need to qualify the judgments reached in the text on the "efficiency" of the training sponsored by MITCE.

The increases in average net earnings levels associated with training in the survey period provided the basis for the estimates of the allocative benefits from training over the remainder of the working lifetimes of trainees. In the text, the allocative benefits from training in the survey period were defined as the average increases in annual earnings levels associated with training, provided that such increases in annual earnings levels were in part attributable to significant increases in average hourly earnings levels. The first three columns in Table E1 reproduce the regression coefficients (from the analysis in Chapter III) which were used in deriving our estimates of the allocative benefits from training in the survey period. The regression coefficients show the net amounts by which average weekly earnings, hours worked per week, and hourly earnings of trainees exceeded the comparable figures for nontrainees in the after-training period. It can be seen that the increases in average weekly earnings levels associated with the training of the various categories of MITCE clients distinguished in Table E1 were made up to a significant extent of increases in average hourly earnings levels. Thus, in our text, the annual allocative benefits from training were

Table E1: Net Regression Coefficients and Annual Allocative Benefits from Training in the Survey Period

Training category	Net regression coefficients			Annual benefits as calculated in our text (dollars)	Annual benefits following Morgan and David (dollars)
	Weekly earnings (dollars)	Hours worked per week	Hourly earnings (cents)		
Female on-the-job trainees	14.54**	7.74*	17.6**	756	352
Male on-the-job trainees	7.39**	0.92	19.2**	384	384
Male institutional trainees	8.25**	2.14	22.9**	429	458
All MITCE trainees	8.32**	2.09**	17.2**	433	344

* Significant at the .05 level.
** Significant at the .01 level.

regarded as the *entire* net increase in annual earnings levels associated with training. To obtain the estimates of the annual allocative benefits from training in the survey period shown in the fourth column of Table E1, the net weekly earnings coefficients associated with the training of the various categories of MITCE clients were simply multiplied by 52.

The criterion employed in the text to measure the allocative benefits from training in the survey period is rather more stringent than that employed in all other published benefit-cost analyses of training programs. Other benefit-cost analysts have regarded the allocative benefits from training programs as being the average increases in annual earnings levels associated with training, regardless of whether or not training was associated with significant increases in average hourly earnings levels. Of course, this criterion leads to the same estimates of the allocative benefits from training MITCE clients as the criterion actually used in our text. However, as was noted in Chapter II, past analyses have not shown that training programs led to *any* allocative benefits to society by the criterion adopted in our text. The increases in average annual earnings levels associated with the training programs studied in other benefit-cost analyses appear to have been entirely attributable to the increased employment of trainees, and not to increases in the average hourly earnings levels of trainees.

It is nevertheless possible to estimate the allocative benefits from training on a more stringent basis than that employed in our text. For instance, in their research on the rate of return to education, Morgan and David take the position that the increases in mean annual earnings levels associated with education only represent genuine allocative benefits to society to the extent that such increases in annual earnings levels are *entirely* attributable to increases in the mean hourly earnings levels of the educated. To calculate the allocative benefits from training MITCE clients according to the criterion of Morgan and David, one simply assumes that in an ideal world all members of the labor force would be fully employed and would have 2,000 hours of work per year.[1] As shown in the fifth column of Table E1, the annual allocative benefits from training in the survey period would therefore be 2,000 times the net increase in average hourly earnings levels associated with training.

The estimates of the allocative benefits from training in the fourth and fifth columns of Table E1 provide an interesting contrast. The regression coefficients in Table E1 indicate the sources of any differences in these estimates. Thus the regression coefficients indicate that for male trainees, the net increases in average weekly earnings levels associated with training were attributable to wage effects. Training was not associated with significant employment effects for these MITCE clients. Thus it was not to be expected that there would be great differences in the estimates of the allocative benefits in the survey period arising from the training of men, whether the basis for calculation of allocative benefits was that proposed by Morgan and David or that used in our text.

---

1. See "Education and Income", pp. 432-33.

On the other hand, the regression coefficients in Table E1 indicate that the net increases in average weekly earnings levels associated with on-the-job training for women were attributable to both significant wage and employment effects. The fact that the average weekly earnings increases associated with the training of all MITCE clients were in part attributable to significant employment effects must also be traced to the significant employment effects associated with on-the-job training for women. Using the criterion employed in the text, the allocative benefits in the survey period from on-the-job training for women and from training all MITCE clients were equal to the average annual increases in earnings associated with training. However, it was to be expected that use of the criterion advocated by Morgan and David would result in substantially lower estimates of the allocative benefits from training these categories of MITCE clients, since the employment effects associated with training in the survey period would be ignored.

The two sets of estimates of the annual allocative benefits from training in the survey period — that used in our text and that derived according to the criterion of Morgan and David — were next employed to obtain the estimates in Tables E2 and E3 of the total allocative benefits from training over the remainder of the working lifetimes of trainees. Tables E2 and E3 also reveal the effects on the total allocative benefits from training of varying the social discount rate used in converting future earnings streams to present values, and of varying the assumption as to the rate of growth in future earnings levels arising from increased productivity in the economy. In deriving the estimates in Chapter IV of the allocative benefits from training MITCE clients, it was assumed that the rate of growth in earnings of a labor force of "constant quality" would be 1.8 per cent per annum, and a social discount rate of 10 per cent per year was used to convert future earnings streams to their present values. In Tables E2 and E3, estimates of the allocative benefits from training are also derived using social discount rates of 8 and 12 per cent per annum, and annual rates of growth of earnings levels of 0, 1 and 2 per cent. The range of values for the social discount rate encompasses most of the estimates of academic economists testifying before Joint Economic Committee Hearings in 1967-68. The alternative assumptions concerning the future growth in earnings levels arising from increases in productivity were those employed by Becker in a similar sensitivity analysis dealing with the rate of return to education.[2]

The Results of the Sensitivity Analysis

One of the main conclusions reached in Chapter IV was that the training of all MITCE clients considered collectively, on-the-job training for male and female MITCE clients, and institutional training for male MITCE clients

---

2.   *Human Capital*, p. 76.

Table E2: Allocative Benefits and Benefit-Cost Ratios for MITCE Training Categories under Alternative Assumptions Concerning Social Discount Rates and Secular Rates of Growth in Earnings:

Benefits Projected Equal the Annual Increase in Earnings Associated with Training in the Survey Period

Training category and social discount rates	Allocative benefits from training (dollars)				Allocative benefit-cost ratios from training			
	Annual rates of growth in earnings (per cent)				Annual rates of growth in earnings (per cent)			
	0	1.0	1.8	2.0	0	1.0	1.8	2.0
Female on-the-job trainees Social discount rates: (per cent)								
8	8228	9083	9870	10082	6.93	7.65	8.32	8.49
10	6902	7536	8113	8268	5.81	6.35	6.83	6.97
12	5912	6395	6830	6946	4.98	5.39	5.75	5.85
Male on-the-job trainees Social discount rates: (per cent)								
8	4070	4482	4860	4962	3.30	3.64	3.94	4.02
10	3428	3735	4014	4089	2.78	3.03	3.26	3.32
12	2946	3181	3392	3449	2.39	2.58	2.75	2.80
Male institutional trainees Social discount rates: (per cent)								
8	4457	4892	5289	5395	1.76	1.93	2.09	2.13
10	3772	4100	4396	4476	1.49	1.62	1.74	1.77
12	3252	3506	3733	3793	1.29	1.39	1.48	1.50
All MITCE trainees Social discount rates: (per cent)								
8	4688	5173	5618	5739	3.12	3.44	3.74	3.82
10	3936	4296	4623	4711	2.62	2.86	3.08	3.13
12	3373	3647	3894	3960	2.24	2.43	2.59	2.63

Table E3: Allocative Benefits and Benefit-Cost Ratios for MITCE Training Categories under Alternative Assumptions Concerning Social Discount Rates and Secular Rates of Growth in Earnings:

Benefits to Training in the Survey Period Calculated by the Method of Morgan and David

Training category and social discount rates	Allocative benefits from training (dollars)				Allocative benefit-cost ratios from training			
	Annual rates of growth in earnings (per cent)				Annual rates of growth in earnings (per cent)			
	0	1.0	1.8	2.0	0	1.0	1.8	2.0
Female on-the-job trainees Social discount rates: (per cent)								
8	3831	4229	4595	4694	3.23	3.56	3.87	3.95
10	3214	3509	3778	3850	2.71	2.96	3.18	3.24
12	2753	2978	3180	3234	2.32	2.51	2.68	2.72
Male on-the-job trainees Social discount rates: (per cent)								
8	4070	4482	4860	4962	3.30	3.64	3.94	4.02
10	3428	3735	4014	4089	2.78	3.03	3.26	3.32
12	2946	3181	3392	3449	2.39	2.58	2.75	2.80
Male institutional trainees Social discount rates: (per cent)								
8	4759	5223	5646	5760	1.88	2.06	2.23	2.28
10	4027	4377	4694	4778	1.59	1.73	1.86	1.89
12	3472	3743	3985	4050	1.37	1.48	1.58	1.60
All MITCE trainees Social discount rates: (per cent)								
8	3725	4110	4464	4559	2.48	2.73	2.97	3.03
10	3127	3413	3673	3742	2.08	2.27	2.44	2.49
12	2680	2898	3094	3146	1.78	1.93	2.06	2.09

represented an efficient use of society's resources. The alternative estimates of the allocative benefits from training derived in this appendix provide additional support for this conclusion; for all of these categories of MITCE trainees, the lowest estimates of the allocative benefits from training in Tables E2 and E3 still exceed the costs of training by considerable margins.

However, the criterion used in our text and the criterion developed from the work of Morgan and David in some cases lead to important differences in the estimates of the allocative benefits and benefit-cost ratios from training the various categories of MITCE clients. Substituting the criterion of Morgan and David for the criterion employed in our text, the allocative benefits from on-the-job training for men are unchanged, the allocative benefits from institutional training for men are raised slightly, the allocative benefits from training all MITCE clients are reduced by roughly one-fifth, and the allocative benefits from on-the-job training for women are reduced by roughly one-half. Considering both the allocative benefits and costs of training, the Morgan and David criterion suggests that on-the-job training for men was the most efficient category of training sponsored by MITCE. On the other hand, if the allocative benefits from training are measured by the criterion adopted in our text, on-the-job training for women appears to be the most efficient category of training sponsored by MITCE.

APPENDIX F

THE SURVEY QUESTIONNAIRE

To simplify presentation, three changes have been made in the structure of the questionnaire originally administered in the survey of MITCE clients. In the first place, the ordering of the questionnaire has been altered so that questions on related topics are grouped together. The original numbering of the questions has been retained to indicate where such changes in the ordering of questions have been made. Secondly, most of the provisions for responses in the original questionnaire have been omitted. Response categories are specified only where the interviewer was required to obtain specific dates or to classify an answer among several mutually exclusive categories. Even in these cases, however, response categories are not specified if they are explicit in the wording of a question or in instructions to the interviewer. Nor are responses specified where questions required simple "yes", "no" or "don't know" answers. Finally, some questions have been omitted which were designed to obtain more detailed information than was given in initial responses to questions. Such "contingent" questions were always asked, for instance, if the respondent was unable to supply specific dates for periods when he was ill, unemployed, not in the labor force, changed jobs, or had changes in his hours of work or wage rates.[1]

Unless otherwise indicated in instructions to the interviewer or in the subheadings of the questionnaire, the questions were addressed to all respondents. Instructions to the interviewer are capitalized. Alternative ways of wording questions are indicated by parentheses or slashes *within* questions. Response categories are given in parentheses *following* a question.

The writer would like to thank the following individuals and institutions for permission to use material contained in the questionnaire: Professors Michael E. Borus and Einar Hardin of Michigan State University; Gerald G. Somers, Director of the Ford Foundation Project for Evaluation of Retraining of Unemployed Workers; and the Survey Research Center, University of Michigan.

---

1. To illustrate the procedure involved, the respondent was asked in question G12 to supply dates for periods when he was absent from work owing to illness. If he was only able to state the month and year in which an illness occurred, this information was recorded. He was then asked how many weeks he was away from work on this occasion, and this information was also recorded.

Appendix F

Respondent Identification

Now, first of all, could you tell me whether I have your name and address right?

Name	(Last)	(First)	(Middle)

Address

BY OBSERVATION ONLY: DO NOT ASK

A 1. Sex of Respondent. (male; female)
A 2. Race of Respondent. (Negro; Indian; Caucasian)

ASK ALL RESPONDENTS

A 3. Now, as I understand it, MITCE first tried to get people around here interested in training over a year ago. When did they first speak to you about training? In what month and year was this?
A 4. Did you get any training through MITCE?

Training History for MITCE Trainees

B 1. What was the main reason you took this training? What did you think you would get out of it? (wanted to shift to a different industry and make more money in the future; wanted to do better in the industry he was in; the money offered during training was good; wanted to get a job in the off-season of the farm)
B 2. What was the second most important reason you took this training? (ENTER CODE FROM B1.)
B 3. What type of training did you get: on-the-job training, or training in a school or community college?
B 4. What was the name of the school/business in which you were trained? In what town was this?
B 5. (IF OJT)* About how many people would you say worked in the business in which
and you were trained? On the average, how many hours a week did you work at your
B 11. training job?
B 6. For what kind of job was the training you got meant to prepare you? What did they train you to do?
B 7. In what industry or line of business would you normally do this job?
B 8. Did MITCE give you a choice of training for different kinds of jobs?
B 9. *At the time you decided to take this training,* did you feel that training for some other kind of work would have been more useful to you? (IF YES) For what kind of a job would you have liked to have been trained? In what industry or line of business would you normally do this job?
B 10. When did the training you got start? In what month and year?
B 12. How long was this training supposed to be? How many weeks was it meant to run for?
B 13. Did you finish this training?

---

* OJT = on-the-job trainee.

ASK ALL MITCE TRAINEES WHO DID NOT FINISH TRAINING

B 14. How many weeks of training did you finish?
B 15. Did you quit the training on your own, or did the employer/school let you go?
B 16. Why did you quit the training, or why did they say they were letting you go? (got a job; insufficient pay or allowances; moved from area; had to care for family; pregnancy of trainee; illness of trainee; went back to school; transportation problems; entered military service; didn't like hours of training; lost interest; disliked training officials/employer; couldn't adjust to training/work; poor attendance; lack of progress; misconduct; alcoholism; committed to an institution; business failed or changed ownership)

ASK ALL MITCE TRAINEES, DEPENDING ON CATEGORY

B 17.
–   (IF OJT AND COMPLETED TRAINING) Now going to the time when you had
B 19. finished training. When did you leave your training job? (month, day, year) Did you quit the training job on your own or did they let you go? Why did you leave your training job, or why did they say they were letting you go? (ENTER CODE FROM B16.)
B 20. (IF OJT AND DID NOT FINISH TRAINING OR IF AN INSTITUTIONAL TRAINEE) When did you start working again? Was it before you left the training course (job) or after you left the training course (job)?
B 21.
–   How many weeks before/after you left the training was it when you started
B 23. working again? (IF TWO OR MORE WEEKS AFTER TRAINING) Of this time, how many weeks were you *not* available for work? Why weren't you available for work these weeks?
B 24. Now about the next full-time job you got after you left your training job (course). Did MITCE help get you this job? (IF YES) When did MITCE tell you about this job; before training began, during training, or after training?

Costs of MITCE Trainees

C 1. Now, I would like to ask you a few questions about the costs or expenses you had in connection with this training. First, did you have to move into town to get this training? (IF YES) What did this move cost you, in your fare and moving expenses?
C 2. How many miles did you have to travel each day to take the training?
C 3. How much did this travel cost you per day or per week?
C 4. (IF AN INSTITUTIONAL TRAINEE) Did you get a transportation or mileage allowance while you were in training? (IF YES) How much did this allowance come to, per week?
C 5. At the time you took the training, could you have gotten a job somewhere else? (IF YES) About how many miles would you have had to travel each day to get to this job?
C 6. Did you have to buy any books, tools, or special work clothing in connection with this training? (IF YES) How much did they cost you? Have you been able to use them since you took the training?
C 7. Did you have any other costs that we haven't already mentioned for this training? (IF YES) What were these costs for? How much did these costs amount to? Was this per day, per week, for the total time you were in training, or what?
C 8. (IF AN INSTITUTIONAL TRAINEE) What was your gross training allowance per week, while you were in training? What were you paid per week before any deductions were taken out? (IF OJT) When you started this training what was your gross pay per hour, before any deductions or taxes were taken out?
C 9. Did you get any pay raises or cuts while you were in training? (IF YES) How many raises or cuts did you get?

ENTER ORIGINAL RATE OF PAY. THEN ASK THE FOLLOWING QUESTIONS *FOR EACH PAY CHANGE* AND ENTER THE RESPONSES.

When was your rate of pay first (next) changed? (month, day, year) What was your new rate of pay?

Training from Agencies Other Than MITCE

D 1. Have any of the following agencies ever enrolled you in training jobs or courses set
— up to teach skills to *unemployed or underemployed workers:* the Employment
D 3. Security Commission of North Carolina; the County Welfare Department; (name of the local community action program); the public employment service of another state; or any other government agency except for the armed services? (IF YES) How many on-the-job training courses or training courses in schools did you get from the agencies we mentioned?

ASK QUESTIONS D4 - D12 FOR EACH INSTANCE OF TRAINING INDICATED IN D1 - D3.

D 4. What type of training was this? (on-the-job training; full-time training in a separate school; part-time training in a separate school i.e. took up less than 20 hours/week)
D 5. What was the name of the agency which got you into the training? (E.S.C. of North Carolina; County Welfare Department; community action program; public employment service of another state)
D 6. Where did you get this training? (town or county, and state)
D 7. When did this training start? (month, year)
D 8. For what type of job was this training meant to prepare you? What did it teach you to do?
D 9. In what industry or line of business would you normally do this job?
D 10. How long in weeks was this training meant to be for?
D10a. How many hours a week did you have to spend in the training course or job?
D 11. Did you finish the training?
D 12. (IF NO TO D11) For how many weeks were you in training?

Information from MITCE and the N.C. Employment Security Commission

D 13. Let's go back to the time when MITCE first talked to you about training. What kinds of training did they talk to you about? (on-the-job training only; training in a school or community college only; or both)
D 14. At that time, did MITCE tell you whether you would get any allowances if you went into a training course in a school? (told he would get allowances; told he would not get allowances; not told whether he would get allowances; (IF TOLD HE WOULD GET ALLOWANCES) What kind of allowances were you told you would get? (IF TOLD HE WOULD NOT GET ALLOWANCES) Did they tell you why you wouldn't get any allowances?)
D 15. Did you have a choice between going into on-the-job training or into a training course in a school? (IF YES) Why did you choose the type of training you took rather than the other type?
D 16. Now, have you ever tried to get a job through the local offices of the Employment Security Commission — the State Employment Office? (IF YES) How did you get to know that you can find jobs at the State Employment Office? Who told you or took you there? Has the E.S.C. ever helped you to find a job? (IF YES) Have you ever taken a job they helped you to find?

ASK ALL RESPONDENTS WHO WERE *NOT* MITCE TRAINEES

E 1. When MITCE was talking to you, were you interested in getting any training? (IF YES ASK E2 THROUGH E6) (IF NO) Why was that? What was the main reason? (PROBE FOR DETAILED RESPONSE. THEN GO TO F1)

E 2. What was the main reason you were interested in getting training? (wanted to shift to a different occupation and make more money in the future; wanted to do better in the occupation he was in; the money offered during training was good; wanted to get a job in the off-season of the farm)

E 3. What was the second most important reason you were interested in getting training? (ENTER CODE FROM E2)

E 4. For what kind of job were you interested in being trained?

E 5. In what industry or line of business would you normally do this job?

E 6. Why didn't you get any training through MITCE?

Demographic Variables

F 1. Now, I'd like to ask you a few questions about yourself. When were you born? (month, year)

F 2. Could you tell me in what state you were born?

F 3. (IF BORN IN NORTH CAROLINA) In what county were you born?

F 4. What is your marital status? (married; widowed; divorced; separated; never married)

F 5. Now, I'd like to ask you a few questions about where you've lived. Since you got your first regular job, how many states have you lived in? Don't include any you might have lived in while in military service.

F 6. (IF ONE STATE) Since you got your first regular job, have you ever lived more than 100 miles from here?

F 7. How many years have you lived in this house?

IF RESPONDENT HAS LIVED SOMEWHERE ELSE IN THE LAST TEN YEARS, ENTER PRESENT TOWN, COUNTY AND STATE OF RESIDENCE. THEN ASK THE FOLLOWING QUESTIONS FOR MOVES BACK TO 1956 AND ENTER RESPONSES.

1. In what year did you move here (there)?
2. Including yourself, how many people moved at your expense?
3. Where did you live before this (that)? (town, county and state)
4. (IF LOCATION NOT CLEAR) Was this in a town, or in the country?
5. Why did you move here (there)? (because parents, spouse, or other relatives moved; to be close to friends or relatives; to get on-the-job training or a training course; to get a better nonfarm job; to get a better farm or farm job; in connection with military service; to get better housing; because dissatisfied where was)

Respondent's Family

F 8. Now, about your family when you were growing up. How many grades of school or years of college did your father finish?

F 9. (IF GRADE SCHOOL OR DOESN'T KNOW) Could he read *and* write?

F 10. What would you say his main job was while you were in grade school?

F 11. In what industry or line of business did he normally do this job?

F 12. Now about your mother: How many grades of school or years of college did she finish?

F 13. (IF GRADE SCHOOL OR DOESN'T KNOW) Could she read *and* write?

F 14. How many brothers and sisters did you have?

Appendix F

Health

F 15. — F 17. Now, about your health. Do you have an illness, injury or health problem which limits the work you can do, and might matter to an employer? (IF YES) How would you describe this problem? Has it arisen in the last four years, or did it start before this time? (IF AFTER) When did it start? In what month and year?

F 18. Now, about your own schooling. How many grades of school or years of college did you finish?

F 19.
F 20. (IF 11 OR 12 GRADES) Did you graduate from high school? (IF NO) Have you passed the High School Equivalency Examination?

F 21. (IF THREE OR MORE YEARS OF COLLEGE) Did you graduate from college?

F 22. Now when you last attended grade school, was this school in the country, or was it in town?

F 23. Were the students in your grade school predominantly nonwhite, or predominantly white?

F 24. What year was it when you last attended grade school?

F 25. What was the name of the grade school you last attended? Where was this school located? In what county and state?

Military Service

F 26. Have you ever been in active military service? (IF YES) Did this military service come before or after the training you got through MITCE? (IF AFTER) While you were in the service, how much could you use of the training you got through MITCE? Would you say all of it, most of it, some of it, or none of it?

F 27. (IF EVER IN MILITARY SERVICE) While you were in the service, did you get any education or training that could be used for *other purposes than strictly military ones*? (IF YES) In what nonmilitary subjects did you get education and training? About how many hours of education and training did you get per week in (each subject)? For about how many weeks was this?

Other Education and Training

F 28. Have you ever had any other education or training we haven't talked about, such as apprenticeships, vocational training courses, correspondence courses, college courses or general adult education courses? (IF YES) How many such educational or apprenticeship courses have you taken?

ASK QUESTIONS F29 - F36 FOR EACH COURSE INDICATED IN F28.

F 29. What type of course was this?

F 30. What subjects did you study in the course, or what were you taught to do?

F 31. Was this course provided by an employer of yours?

F 32. When did you start this course? In what month and year?

F 33. How long was this course supposed to be? How many weeks was it meant to run for?

F 34. How many hours a week did you spend in this course?

F 35. Did you finish the course?

F 36. (IF NO TO F35) How long did you stay in the course? For how many weeks did you take it?

Present Labor Force Status

G 1. Now we would like to ask you a few questions about your job experience in the last few years. We want to find out what you have been doing since April, 1964, which should be at least a year before MITCE first got in touch with you. First of all we'd like to know what you were doing most of last week. Were you working?

WORKING		CIRCLE ONE NUMBER	INSTRUCTION COLUMN
Yes	Were you operating a farm as your main job?		
	Yes	1	– GO TO J1
	No Have you been working for this employer or yourself for more than four weeks?		
	Yes	2	– GO TO G2
	No (TREAT AS ODD JOB)	3	– GO TO G37
No	Even though you weren't working last week, did you have a job from which you were temporarily absent?		
	Yes Why weren't you working at this job?		
	on vacation	4	
	had temporary illness	5	– GO TO G2
	industrial dispute	6	
	bad weather	7	
	No Were you looking for work?		
	Yes	8	– GO TO H1
	No Why weren't you looking for work?		
	keeping house	9	
	retired	10	
	going to school	11	– GO TO I1
	long-term illness	12	
	pregnant	13	

Employment History for Occupations Other than Farm Operator

G 2. Did you work for yourself or someone else on this job?
G 3. What was the name of the business you worked for?
G 4. Where was this business located? (town, county and state)
G 5. What kind of work did you do in this job? What did they call your job?
G 6. What did the business (you worked for) do? What industry or line of business were they (you) in?
G 7. When did you start working on this job? (month, day, year) When did you last work at this job? (month, day, year)
G 8. Did you get any training on this job *during special hours or in separate classrooms*? (IF YES) What sort of things were you taught in this training? About how many hours of training did you get?
G 9. (IF MITCE TRAINEE) In this job, how much could you use of the training you got through MITCE? Would you say all of it, most of it, some of it, or none of it?
G 10. (IF MITCE TRAINEE USING TRAINING) Could you have gotten this job without the training you had through MITCE?
G 11. Were you ever away from work for a week or more while you were working at this
– job? (IF YES) How many times were you away from this work for a week or more?
G 12. When was the first (next) time you were away from work? (from month, day, year to month, day, year) Why were you away from work? Did you get any pay from your employer (or union) in connection with this absence? (IF YES) How much did you get before any taxes or deductions were taken out?

Appendix F

G 13.   (IF NOT SELF-EMPLOYED) Were you paid by the hour (H), day (D), week (W), month (M), or on commission (C)?

G 14.   (IF C, SELF-EMPLOYED, OR EMPLOYED ON AN IRREGULAR BASIS) Including all earnings from this job, what were you paid per (H, D, W, OR M) before taxes or deductions were taken out?

G 15.   (IF H, D, W, OR M) When you started working at this job, what were you paid per (H, D, W, OR M) before taxes or deductions were taken out?

G 16.   (IF H, D, W, OR M) Did you get any pay raises or cuts while you were on this job? (IF YES) How many raises or cuts did you get? (ENTER ORIGINAL PAY RATE AND ASK) When was your rate of pay first (next) changed? (month, day, year) What was your new rate of pay?

G 17.   (IF UNABLE TO GET ANSWERS TO G14 - G16) What was the largest amount you earned per week in this job, before any taxes and deductions were taken out? What was the smallest amount you earned per week in this job, before taxes and deductions were taken out? What was the most common amount you earned per week, before taxes and deductions were taken out?

G 18.   How many hours a week did you work when you began this job?

G 19.   While you were working on this job, did the hours you worked ever change? (IF YES) How many times were your hours changed?

G 20.   (IF MORE THAN 3 CHANGES IN HOURS) On the average, how many hours did you work per week?

G 21.   (IF 3 CHANGES IN HOURS OR LESS ENTER ORIGINAL HOURS PER WEEK AND ASK) When were your hours first (next) changed? (month, day, year) How many hours per week did you work next?

G 22.   (IF NOT SELF-EMPLOYED AND WORKED OVER 40 HOURS PER WEEK) Did you receive any overtime pay for working more than 40 hours per week? (IF YES) Did you get time and a half or some other amount for working this overtime? (RECORD AS PROPORTION OF BASE PAY)

G 23.   (IF NOT SELF-EMPLOYED) Were you ever paid more than your basic hourly rate for such things as shift differentials, working on weekends, incentive plans, or production bonuses? (IF YES, RECORD REASON AND ASK) For how many weeks did you get this extra pay? How much did this extra pay amount to, per week?

G 24.   (IF SELF-EMPLOYED) How many employees did you have *apart* from unpaid family members? How many unpaid family members worked with you in this business? (GO TO G37)

ASK G25 THROUGH G36 ONLY IF RESPONDENT WAS NOT SELF-EMPLOYED

G 25.   Did you pay social security on this job? (IF NO) Do you know whether your employer paid *all* the social security contributions?

G 26.   Did you have to join a union to work at this job? (IF YES) What did your union dues cost you and how often did you have to pay them? Did you have to pay an entrance fee to join this union? (IF YES) How much did it cost you?

G 27.   To get this job, did you have to pay a fee to a private employment agency, or pay for a physical examination? (IF YES) How much did it (they) cost you?

G 28.   Did you *have* to buy any tools, equipment or uniforms to work at this job? (IF YES) How much did they cost you? Have you been able to use them on other jobs?

G 29.   Were you entitled to a *paid* annual vacation on this job? (IF YES) How many days of *paid* annual vacation were you entitled to?

G 30.   Were you entitled to any paid sick leave while you were working on this job? (IF YES) How many days of paid sick leave were you entitled to per year?

G 31.   Did the business you were working for have paid holidays on any of these days: New Year's Day, Christmas Day, Easter Monday, Independence Day, Labor Day, Thanksgiving Day, or any other day? (IF YES) How many such paid holidays did this business have?

G 32. Did the business you worked for sponsor or provide any *group life insurance* for its employees? (IF YES) Did you get any of this life insurance? (IF YES) Did the business pay any share of the premium and if so, what did you pay, and what did the business pay? (ENTER AMOUNTS AND RELEVANT TIME PERIODS)

G 33. Did the business you worked for arrange any *group hospitalization insurance* for its employees, such as Blue Cross or Blue Shield? (IF YES) Did you get any of this health insurance? (IF YES) Did the business pay any part of the premium, and if so, what did you pay and what did the business pay? (ENTER AMOUNTS AND RELEVANT TIME PERIODS)

G 34. Did the business you worked for have a retirement or pension plan for its employees? (IF YES) Did you pay into it? (IF YES) What did you pay, and what did the business pay towards this plan? (ENTER AMOUNTS AND RELEVANT TIME PERIODS)

G 35. Did you get any payment *in kind* from this employer, such as free meals or clothing you used outside the job? (IF YES) How many meals did you get per week, and how much did you save by getting them? How much do you think the clothing was worth?

G36. (IF NO LONGER WORKING AT THIS JOB) When you stopped working at this job, did you get any of the following kinds of payments, *in addition* to your last regular pay check: supplemental unemployment benefits (NOTE: NOT UNEMPLOYMENT INSURANCE), severance pay, vacation pay, sickness or disability pay, or workmen's compensation? (IF YES, ENTER AMOUNT RECEIVED)

ASK ALL RESPONDENTS

G 37. While you were working at the main job we've been talking about, from (beginning date in G6) to (ending date in G6), did you have any other jobs? It is important that we know something about these jobs, even if they only took up a few days or a few hours a week. How many odd jobs did you have in this period? (FOR EACH ODD JOB, ASK) What did you do on this job? In what month and year did you start on this job? Were you paid by the hour (H), day (D), or week (W) on this job? What were you paid per (H, D, or W)? How many hours per (D or W) did you work? How many days or weeks did you work at this job? Approximately how much did you earn from this job?

G 38. What were you doing just before this main job we've been talking about? Were you operating a farm as your main job? (IF YES GO TO J1) Were you working for yourself or someone else for more than four weeks? (IF YES GO TO G2) Were you working for yourself or someone else for less than four weeks? (IF YES GO TO G37) Were you unemployed for a while? (IF YES GO TO H1) Were you not working and not looking for work? (IF YES GO TO I1)

Periods of Unemployment

H 1. What were you doing to find a job in this period? (actively searching for a job by registering with an employment agency, contacting prospective employers, checking newspaper ads, using pick-up zone, etc.; not actively searching for a job – GO TO SECTION I, NOT IN LABOR FORCE)

H 2. When did this period of unemployment begin? (month, day, year)

H 3. Was a job offered you during this time which you did not take? (IF YES) Why didn't you take it?

H 4. Did you work at all during this period, even for just a few days or a few hours a week? (IF YES) How many jobs did you have? (GO TO G37 AND ENTER DETAILS)

H 5. What were you doing just before this period of unemployment that we've been talking about? Were you operating a farm as your main job? (IF YES GO TO J1) Were you working for yourself or someone else for more than four weeks? (IF YES

Appendix F

GO TO G2) Were you working for yourself or someone else for less than four weeks? (IF YES GO TO G37) Were you not working and not looking for work? (IF YES GO TO I1)

Periods Not in the Labor Force

I 1. Why weren't you looking for work at this time? (housewife/supported by spouse; retired; going to school; long-term illness; pregnant; in training with MITCE)

I 2. When did this period of not working and not looking for work begin? (month, day, year)

I 3. Did you work at all during this period, even for just a few days or a few hours a week? (IF YES) How many such jobs did you have? (GO TO G37 AND ENTER DETAILS)

I 4. What were you doing just before this period when you were not working and not looking for work? Were you operating a farm as your main job? (IF YES GO TO J1) Were you working for yourself or someone else for more than four weeks? (IF YES, GO TO G2) Were you working for yourself or someone else for less than four weeks? (IF YES, GO TO G37) Were you looking for work? (IF YES GO TO H1)

Self-Employment as Farm Operator

J 1. (IF RESPONDENT HAS INDICATED OPERATING A FARM WAS HIS MAIN JOB) What years have you farmed since 1964? (IF RESPONDENT HAS NOT INDICATED HE WAS OPERATING A FARM) Are you doing any farming of products for sale this year, or have you done any since 1964? (IF YES) What years have you farmed?

ASK J2 - J10 FOR EACH YEAR RESPONDENT WAS A FARM OPERATOR

J 2. What farm product would you say yielded you the most cash income in this year? (tobacco; cotton; cash grains; other field crops; vegetables; fruits and nuts; poultry; dairy products; livestock)

J 3. On the average, about how many hours per week do you think *you* spent on farm work at these times of the year: (a) from January through March; (b) from April through June; (c) from July through September; (d) from October through December?

J 4. Did any other members of your family work on the farm without receiving cash wages? (IF YES) How many of these were over 14 years old, and how many were under 14 years? On the average, about how many hours per week did each adult over 14 years and/or child under 14 years work in these periods: (a) from January through March; (b) from April through June; (c) from July through September; (d) from October through December?

J 5. What was your total income from farming that year? How much did you gross from the sale of all products, after the landlord's share, if any, was taken out? Please include any money you got from crops you placed under commodity loans, or soil bank payments.

J 6. What were your total operating expenses for this year, *not counting living expenses or income taxes?*

J 7. Did you include in your expenses any money that you spent on things that would have lasted for a while, such as tractors, trucks, equipment or buildings? (IF YES) How much went for things like that?

J 8. How much was the livestock and equipment you owned worth? How much would you have gotten if you sold it?

J 9. Did you own any land or buildings on this farm? (IF YES) How much do you think they were worth?

J 10. (IF OPERATING A FARM WAS MAIN JOB) While you were farming in the year we've been talking about, did you work at any other jobs, for yourself or anyone else? (IF YES) How many other jobs did you have? How many of these jobs lasted more than four weeks and were full-time jobs? (ASK G2 - G36 ABOUT SUCH JOBS) How many of these jobs lasted less than four weeks or were part-time jobs? (ASK G37 ABOUT SUCH JOBS)

J 11. What were you doing before this? Were you operating a farm as your main job in (the previous year)? (IF YES GO TO J1) Were you working for yourself or someone else for more than four weeks? (IF YES GO TO G2) Were you working for yourself or someone else for less than four weeks? (IF YES GO TO G37) Were you looking for work? (IF YES GO TO H1) Were you not working and not looking for work? (IF YES GO TO I1)

Housing, Home Production of Food and Dependents

K 1. Now, I have a few questions about your home and family. First, do you own or are you buying this house? Do you rent this place? Do you rent rooms in this place? Are you living with relatives or friends, and helping with the rent? Do you get this place rent free, in connection with your job or farm?

K 2. (IF OWNS OR IS BUYING HOME) About how much do you think it would cost you to rent a house like this around here if you had to furnish it and pay for the utilities, like water, heat and power? (ENTER $ AND TIME PERIOD) About how much do you think a house like this would sell for on today's market? Does that include any farm land or business property? (IF YES) About how much would the *house* sell for?

K 3. (IF RENTS HOUSE OR ROOMS, OR LIVES WITH RELATIVES OR FRIENDS AND CONTRIBUTES TO RENT) About how much rent do you pay? (ENTER $ AND TIME PERIOD) Do you rent this house (these rooms) furnished, or unfurnished?

K 4. (IF RENT-FREE IN CONNECTION WITH JOB OR FARM) About how much do you think it would cost you to rent a place like this around here if you had to furnish it and pay for the utilities like water, heat and power? (ENTER $ AND TIME PERIOD)

K 5. (1) Do you pay for electricity? (IF YES) What is the *average monthly* cost for electricity?

(2) Do you pay for gas? (IF YES) What is the *average monthly* cost for gas?

(3) Do you pay for water? (IF YES) What is the *average monthly* cost for water?

(4) Do you pay for fuels such as oil, coal, kerosene, or wood? (IF YES) About how much do you pay for such fuels per year?

K 6. Do you grow any vegetables, raise animals or poultry for your own food, or anything like that? (IF YES) About how much do you think you save in food bills per week or month by doing this yourself? (ENTER $ AND TIME PERIOD) About how much of your food for the year do you grow or raise yourself? (RECORD FRACTION)

K 7. Now, I'd like to ask you a few questions about other members of your family and household. First, how many dependents do you have? Not counting yourself, how many people depend on you for more than half of their support? How many of these dependents are children under 14 years old? How many of these dependents are age 14 years and older?

Job History of Adult Household Members

K 8. Now, we have a few questions about the work and employment of other members of your household who are 14 years or older. Would you tell me the first names of these persons? (LIST FIRST NAMES AND ASK K9 - K15 FOR EACH PERSON)

Appendix F

K 9.   In what year was (name of first person listed) born?

K 10. What is his/her relationship to you?

K 11. Has he/she been a member of your household since April, 1964? (IF NO) In what year did he/she join your household?

K 12. What was he/she doing last year? (USE G1 TO DETERMINE CODE FOR LABOR FORCE STATUS)

K 13. Has he/she had any paid employment in 1967? (IF YES) About how many weeks has he/she worked? About how much does he/she gross per week?

K 14. Did he/she have any paid employment in 1966? (IF YES) About how many weeks did he/she work? About how much did he/she gross per week?

K 15. Did he/she have any paid employment in 1965? (IF YES) About how many weeks did he/she work? About how much did he/she gross per week?

K 16. Did he/she have any paid employment in 1964? (IF YES) About how many weeks did he/she work? About how much did he/she gross per week?

Unemployment Compensation

L 1.   Have you or anyone else in your household received unemployment compensation from a government agency at any time since April, 1964?

L 2.   (IF YES) Who was this? Anyone else? (LIST FIRST NAMES)

L 3.   When did (first person listed) receive the first benefit check after April 1, 1964? (month, year)

L 4.   When did the benefit checks stop (that time)? (month, year)

L 5.   Why did the benefits stop? (benefits exhausted; still receiving benefits; got a job; was disqualified)

L 6.   How many checks did (name of person) receive?

L 7.   How much did (name of person) receive per week?

L 8.   Did (name of person) receive unemployment benefits at any other time since April, 1964? (IF YES, LIST NAME AGAIN AND REPEAT L3 THROUGH L8. IF NO, ASK L3 THROUGH L8 FOR NEXT PERSON)

Aid from Governmental Agencies

M 1.   Have you or anyone in your household received assistance such as money, surplus food or food stamps, medical care or other things like this from the County Welfare Department or any other government agency since April, 1964?

M 2.   (IF YES) Who was this? Anyone else? (LIST FIRST NAMES)

M 3.   For (first person listed), when did this assistance begin? (month, year)

M 4.   When did it end (that time)? (month, year)

M 5.   From what agency did he receive this assistance? (County Welfare Department; Social Security Administration; military pension)

M 6.   What was the purpose of this assistance? (aid for dependent children, including medical; aid to blind or disabled; aid to aged, including medical)

M 7.   What type of assistance was it? (cash or check; food stamps or surplus food; medical care)

M 8.   What would you say was the money value of all the assistance (name of person) got at this time?

M 9.   Did (name of person) receive help at any other time? (IF YES, LIST NAME AGAIN AND REPEAT M3 THROUGH M9. IF NO ASK M3 THROUGH M9 FOR NEXT PERSON)

Aid from Nongovernmental Agencies

N 1.   Have you or anyone else in your household received assistance of any kind from any private social agency such as the Salvation Army or the Community Chest since April, 1964?

N 2. (IF YES) Who was this? Anyone else? (LIST FIRST NAMES)
N 3. During what period of time did (name of person) receive assistance?
N 4. From what agency did he receive it (that time)?
N 5. What kinds of assistance did he get (that time)?
N 6. What would you say was the money value of all the assistance he received (that time)?
N 7. Did this person receive assistance at any other time since April, 1964? (IF YES, LIST NAME AGAIN AND REPEAT N3 THROUGH N7. IF NO, GO TO NEXT NAME ON LIST)

Aid from Friends and Relatives

O 1. Have you or anyone else in your household received assistance *of any kind* from friends or relatives since April, 1964? We mean such things as free board for yourself, money to help you or your family over rough periods, or food and clothing which weren't Christmas or birthday gifts.
O 2. (IF YES) Who got this help? Anyone else? (LIST FIRST NAMES)
O 3. What kind of help was this? (free board; money; food or clothing)
O 4. During what period of time did (name of person) get this help? From when to when? (month, year) (IF FREE BOARD) For how many weeks did (name of person) get this free board?
O 5. (IF MONEY GIVEN) How much money did (name of person) get? (IF FREE BOARD) How much would you say this free board was worth per week? (IF FOOD OR CLOTHING) What would you say was the money value of this food and clothing (name of person) got?
O 6. Did (name of person) get any other help from friends or relatives at any time since April, 1964? (IF YES, LIST NAME AGAIN AND REPEAT O3 THROUGH O6. IF NO, GO TO NEXT NAME ON LIST AND ASK O3 THROUGH O6)

Planning, Financial Status and Need-Achievement Rating

P 1. Finally, we have a few general questions. First, do you have any life insurance on yourself?
P 2. Do you people have Blue Cross or other hospitalization insurance? (IF YES) Who does this insurance cover? (respondent only; respondent, spouse and children)
P 3. How about savings in banks or savings and loan associations or government bonds? Do you and your family have as much as $500 in such savings? (IF NO) Do you have any savings?
P 4. Some people feel that they can make pretty definite plans for their lives for the next few years. Others feel that they aren't in a position to plan ahead. How about you? Do you feel able to plan ahead or not? Why (not)?
P 5. Do you plan ahead as to what your next major purchases will be, or do you buy things when you have to have them?
P 6. Some people say that people get ahead by their own hard work; others say that lucky breaks or help from other people are most important. What do you think about this?
P 7. We would like to know how people compare occupations. How do you think most people would feel if a boy of theirs chose these types of work?

Appendix F

	Not Happy	Wouldn't Mind	Happy	Very Happy	Delighted
a. Carpenter					
b. Social Worker					
c. Doctor					
d. Night Watchman					
e. Mail Carrier					
f. Bookkeeper					
g. Bus Driver					
h. High School Teacher					
i. Auto Mechanic					
j. Drug Store Owner					

SELECTED BIBLIOGRAPHY

Anderson, W. H. Locke. "Trickling Down: The Relationship Between Economic Growth and the Extent of Poverty Among American Families." *Quarterly Journal of Economics* 78 (November, 1964): 511-24.

Bateman, Worth S. "An Application of Cost-Benefit Analysis to the Work-Experience Program." *American Economic Review* 57 (May, 1967): 80-90.

Baumol, William. "On the Social Rate of Discount." *American Economic Review* 58 (September, 1968): 788-802.

Becker, Gary S. *Human Capital.* New York: National Bureau of Economic Research, 1964.

Blank, David M. and Stigler, George J. *The Demand and Supply of Scientific Personnel.* New York: National Bureau of Economic Research, 1957.

Blaug, M. "An Economic Interpretation of the Private Demand for Education." *Economica* 33 (May, 1966): 166-82.

_____. *The Economics of Education.* 2 vols. Harmondsworth, England: Penguin Books, 1968.

_____. "The Rate of Return on Investment in Education." *The Manchester Journal* 33 (September, 1965): 205-51.

Blitz, Rudolf C. "The Nation's Educational Outlay." In U.S. Department of Health, Education and Welfare, Office of Education, *Economics of Higher Education,* edited by Selma J. Mushkin, pp. 147-69. Washington, D.C.: Government Printing Office, 1962.

Borus, Michael E. "A Benefit-Cost Analysis of the Economic Effectiveness of Retraining the Unemployed." *Yale Economic Essays* 4 (Fall, 1964): 371-429.

_____. *The Economic Effectiveness of Retraining the Unemployed.* Research Report to the Federal Reserve Bank of Boston, No. 35. Boston: The Federal Reserve Bank of Boston, 1966.

_____. "The Effects of Retraining the Unemployed in Connecticut." In *Retraining the Unemployed,* edited by Gerald G. Somers, pp. 125-48. Madison, Wis.: University of Wisconsin Press, 1968.

_____. "Time Trends in the Benefits from Retraining in Connecticut." In *Industrial Relations Research Association, Proceedings of the Twentieth Annual Winter Meeting,* pp. 36-46. Madison, Wis., 1967.

Bowles, Samuel. "Aggregation of Labor Inputs in the Economics of Growth and Planning: Experiments with a Two-Level CES Function." *Journal of Political Economy* 78 (February, 1970): 68-81.

_____. *Planning Educational Systems for Economic Growth.* Cambridge, Mass.: Harvard University Press, 1969.

_____. "Towards an Educational Production Function." In *Education, Income, and Human Capital,* edited by W. Lee Hansen, pp. 11-61. New York: National Bureau of Economic Research, 1970.

Bibliography

Brazer, Harvey E. and David, Martin. "Social and Economic Determinants of the Demand for Education." In U.S. Department of Health, Education and Welfare, Office of Education, *Economics of Higher Education,* edited by Selma J. Mushkin, pp. 21-42. Washington, D.C.: Government Printing Office, 1962.

Cain, Glen G. *Benefit-Cost Estimates for Job Corps.* Madison, Wis.: Institute for Research on Poverty, The University of Wisconsin, 1967.

_____, and Hollister, Robinson W. "Evaluating Manpower Programs for the Disadvantaged." In *Cost-Benefit Analysis of Manpower Policies,* edited by G. G. Somers and W. D. Wood, pp. 119-51. Kingston, Ontario: Industrial Relations Centre, Queen's University, 1970.

_____, and Somers, Gerald G. "Retraining the Disadvantaged Worker." In *Research in Vocational Education,* edited by Cathleen Quirk and Carol Sheehan, pp. 27-44. Madison, Wis.: Center for Studies in Vocational and Technical Education, The University of Wisconsin, 1967.

_____, and Stromsdorfer, Ernst W. "An Economic Evaluation of Government Retraining Programs in West Virginia." In *Retraining the Unemployed,* edited by Gerald G. Somers, pp. 299-335. Madison, Wis.: University of Wisconsin Press, 1968.

Carol, Arthur, and Parry, Samuel. "The Economic Rationale of Occupational Choice." *Industrial and Labor Relations Review* 21 (January, 1968): 183-96.

Carroll, Adger B. and Ihnen, Loren A. "Costs and Returns for Two Years of Postsecondary Technical Schooling: A Pilot Study." *Journal of Political Economy* 75 (December, 1967): 862-73.

Chase, Samuel B. Jr., ed. *Problems in Public Expenditure Analysis.* Washington, D.C.: The Brookings Institution, 1968.

Colberg, Marshall R. *Human Capital in Southern Development, 1939-1963.* Chapel Hill, N.C.: University of North Carolina Press, 1965.

Eckaus, R. S. "Economic Criteria for Education and Training." *Review of Economics and Statistics* 46 (May, 1964): 181-90.

Eckstein, Otto. "A Survey of the Theory of Public Expenditure Criteria." In *Public Finances: Needs, Sources and Utilization,* edited by James M. Buchanan, pp. 439-94. National Bureau of Economic Research Special Conference Series No. 12. Princeton, N.J.: Princeton University Press, 1961.

Enke, Stephen. "The Economic Aspects of Slowing Population Growth." *The Economic Journal* 76 (March, 1966): 44-56.

Esser, George H. Jr. "What the Rural Poor Want." Mimeographed. Durham, N.C.: The North Carolina Fund, 1967.

Finegan, Aldrich T. "Hours of Work in the United States: A Cross-Sectional Analysis." *Journal of Political Economy* 70 (October, 1962): 452-70.

Fleisher, Belton M. "The Effect of Income on Delinquency." *American Economic Review* 56 (March, 1966): 118-37.

_____. "The Effect of Income on Delinquency: Reply." *American Economic Review* 60 (March, 1970): 257.

Friedman, Rose D. *Poverty: Definition and Perspective.* Washington, D.C.: American Enterprise Institute for Public Policy Research, 1965.

Gibbard, Harold A. and Somers, Gerald G. "Government Retraining of the Unemployed in West Virginia." In *Retraining the Unemployed,* edited by Gerald G. Somers, pp. 17-124. Madison, Wis.: University of Wisconsin Press, 1968.

Bibliography

Gilmour, Edwin C. "The Facts about Rural Poverty." Address to the National Association for Community Development Conference on Rural Poverty, Washington, D.C., 1967.

Green, Christopher. *Negative Taxes and the Poverty Problem.* Washington, D.C.: The Brookings Institution, 1967.

Griliches, Zvi. "Notes on the Role of Education in Production Functions and Growth Accounting." In *Education, Income and Human Capital,* edited by W. Lee Hansen, pp. 71-115. New York: National Bureau of Economic Research, 1970.

————. "Research Costs and Social Returns: Hybrid Corn and Related Innovations." *Journal of Political Economy* 66 (October, 1958): 419-31.

Hanoch, Giora. "An Economic Analysis of Earnings and Schooling." *Journal of Human Resources* 2 (Summer, 1967): 310-29.

Hansen, Morris H., Hurwitz, William N., and Madow, William G. *Sample Survey Methods and Theory.* New York: John Wiley and Sons, 1964.

Hansen, W. Lee, Weisbrod, Burton A., and Scanlon, William. "Schooling and Earnings of Low Achievers." *American Economic Review* 60 (June, 1970): 409-18.

Hardin, Einar. "Benefit-Cost Analysis of Occupational Training Programs." In *Cost-Benefit Analysis of Manpower Policies,* edited by G. G. Somers and W. D. Wood, pp. 97-118. Kingston, Ontario: Industrial Relations Centre, Queen's University, 1970.

Houthakker, H.S. "Education and Income." *Review of Economics and Statistics* 41 (February, 1959): 24-28.

Hunt, Shane J. "Income Determinants for College Graduates and the Return to Educational Investment." *Yale Economic Essays* 3 (Fall, 1963): 304-57.

The Institute for Defense Analyses. *Federal Poverty Programs: Assessment and Recommendations.* Report R-116. Arlington, Va.: The Institute for Defense Analyses, 1966.

Keats, John. *The Sheepskin Psychosis.* Philadelphia: Lippincott, 1965.

Lampman, Robert J. "Approaches to the Reduction of Poverty." *American Economic Review* 55 (May, 1965): 521-29.

Levine, Robert A. "Evaluation of Economic Opportunity Programs: A Progress Report." *American Statistical Association, Proceedings of the Social Statistics Section, 126th Annual Meeting, 1966,* pp. 342-51. Los Angeles, Calif., 1966.

Maass, Arthur. "Benefit-Cost Analysis: Its Relevance to Public Investment Decisions." *Quarterly Journal of Economics* 80 (May, 1966): 208-26.

Machlup, Fritz. *The Production and Distribution of Knowledge in the United States.* Princeton, N.J.: Princeton University Press, 1962.

Main, Earl D. "A Nationwide Evaluation of MDTA Institutional Job Training." *Journal of Human Resources* 3 (Spring, 1968): 159-70.

The Manpower Development and Training Act of 1962, as amended (42 U.S. Code 2571-2620).

Manpower Improvement through Community Effort. *Final Report under U.S. Department of Labor Contract No. 82-32-30.* Durham, N.C.: The North Carolina Fund, 1967.

Marglin, Stephen A. "Objectives of Water-Resource Development: A General Statement." In *Design of Water Resource Systems,* by Arthur Maass *et al.,* pp. 17-87. Cambridge, Mass.: Harvard University Press, 1962.

Bibliography

Marshall, Alfred. *Principles of Economics.* 8th ed. London: Macmillan, 1966.

McLelland, David S. *The Achieving Society.* Princeton, N.J.: Van Nostrand, 1961.

Mincer, Jacob. "The Distribution of Labor Incomes: A Survey with Special Reference to the Human Capital Approach." *Journal of Economic Literature* 8 (March, 1970): 1-26.

————. "On-the-Job Training: Costs, Returns, and Implications." *Journal of Political Economy* 70 (Supplement, October, 1962): 50-79.

Morgan, James N. "The Achievement Motive and Economic Behavior." *Economic Development and Cultural Change* 12 (April, 1964): 243-67.

————, et al. *Income and Welfare in the United States.* New York: McGraw-Hill, 1962.

————, and David, Martin. "Education and Income." *Quarterly Journal of Economics* 77 (August, 1963): 423-37.

————, and Sirageldin, Ismail. "A Note on the Quality Dimension of Education." *Journal of Political Economy* 76 (September, 1968): 1069-77.

————, and Sonquist, John A. "Problems in the Analysis of Survey Data and a Proposal." *Journal of the American Statistical Association* 58 (June, 1963): 415-34.

Musgrave, Richard A. "Cost-Benefit Analysis and the Theory of Public Finance." *Journal of Economic Literature* 7 (September, 1969): 797-806.

Orshansky, Mollie. "Counting the Poor: Another Look at the Poverty Profile." *The Social Security Bulletin* 28 (January, 1965): 3-29.

Page, David A. "Retraining under the Manpower Development Act: A Cost-Benefit Analysis." *Public Policy* 13 (1964): 257-67.

Planning Research Corporation. *Cost Effectiveness Analysis of On-the-Job and Institutional Training Courses.* PRC D-1297. Washington, D.C.: Planning Research Corporation, 1967.

Prest, A.R. and Turvey, R. "Cost-Benefit Analysis: A Survey." *The Economic Journal* 75 (December, 1965): 683-735.

Rees, Albert. "Review of 'Human Capital', by Gary S. Becker." *American Economic Review* 55 (September, 1965): 958-60.

Ribich, Thomas I. *Education and Poverty.* Washington, D.C.: The Brookings Institution, 1968.

Schultz, Theodore W. "Capital Formation by Education." *Journal of Political Economy* 68 (December, 1960): 571-83.

————. "Investing in Poor People: An Economist's View." *American Economic Review* 55 (May, 1965): 510-20.

————. "Investment in Human Capital." *American Economic Review* 51 (March, 1961): 1-17.

Schwartzman, David. "The Contribution of Education to the Quality of Labor, 1929-1963." *American Economic Review* 58 (June, 1968): 508-14.

Scoville, James G. "Education and Training Requirements for Occupations." *Review of Economics and Statistics* 48 (November, 1966): 387-94.

Selowsky, Marcelo. "On the Measurement of Education's Contribution to Growth." *Quarterly Journal of Economics* 83 (August, 1969): 449-63.

Sewell, David. "Some Implications of Employment Trends in North Carolina, 1950-1960." Mimeographed. Durham, N.C.: The North Carolina Fund, 1966.

Simons, Henry. *Economic Policy for a Free Society.* Chicago: University of Chicago Press, 1948.

Solie, Richard J. "Employment Effects of Retraining the Unemployed." *Industrial and Labor Relations Review* 21 (January, 1968): 210-25.

Solow, Robert M. "Review of 'Human Capital', by Gary S. Becker." *Journal of Political Economy* 73 (October, 1965): 552-53.

Somers, Gerald G. "Evaluation of Work Experience and Training of Older Workers." Unpublished report to the National Council on the Aging, University of Wisconsin. Madison, Wis.: Industrial Relations Research Institute, 1967.

_____, and McKechnie, Graeme H. "Vocational Retraining Programs for the Unemployed." In *Industrial Relations Research Association, Proceedings of the Twentieth Annual Winter Meeting,* pp. 25-35. Madison, Wis., 1967.

_____, and Stromsdorfer, Ernst W. "Benefit-Cost Analysis of Manpower Retraining." In *Industrial Relations Research Association, Proceedings of the Seventeenth Annual Meeting,* pp. 172-85. Madison, Wis., 1964.

Stigler, George J. "Imperfections in the Capital Market." *Journal of Political Economy* 75 (June, 1967): 287-92.

Strasser, Arnold. "The Changing Structure of Compensation." *Monthly Labor Review* 89 (September, 1966): 953-58.

Stromsdorfer, Ernst. "Determinants of Economic Success in Retraining the Unemployed: The West Virginia Experience." *Journal of Human Resources* 3 (Spring, 1968): 139-58.

Suits, Daniel B. "The Use of Dummy Variables in Regression Equations." *Journal of the American Statistical Association* 52 (December, 1967): 548-51.

Taussig, Michael K. "An Economic Analysis of Vocational Education in the New York City High Schools." *Journal of Human Resources* 3 (Supplement, 1968): 59-87.

Thurow, Lester C. "The Causes of Poverty." *Quarterly Journal of Economics* 71 (February, 1967): 39-57.

Tobin, James. "On Improving the Economic Status of the Negro." *Daedalus* 94 (Fall, 1965): 878-99.

U.S. Congress. Joint Economic Committee. Subcommittee on Economy in Government. *Economic Analysis of Public Investment Decisions: Interest Rate Policy and Discounting Analysis: Hearings.* 90th Cong., 2nd sess., 1968.

_____. Joint Economic Committee. Subcommittee on Economy in Government. *The Planning-Programming-Budgeting System: Progress and Potentials: Hearings.* 90th Cong., 1st sess., 1967.

_____. Senate. Committee on Labor and Public Welfare. Subcommittee on Employment, Manpower and Poverty. "Manpower Programs in the Antipoverty Effort," by Garth L. Mangum. In *Examination of the War on Poverty,* pp. 235 *et seq.* Staff and Consultants Reports, vol. II. 90th Cong., 1st sess., 1967.

U.S. Department of Agriculture. Economic Research Service. *Net Migration of the Population, 1950-60, by Age, Sex, and Color.* Vol. I. Washington, D.C.: Government Printing Office, 1965.

Bibliography

U.S. Department of Commerce. Bureau of the Census. *Long Term Economic Growth.* Washington, D.C.: Government Printing Office, 1966.

_____. Bureau of the Census. *Present Value of Estimated Lifetime Earnings,* by Herman P. Miller and Richard A. Hornseth. Technical Paper No. 16. Washington, D.C.: Government Printing Office, 1967.

_____. Bureau of the Census. *Statistical Abstract of the United States, 1967.* Washington, D.C.: Government Printing Office, 1967.

_____. Bureau of the Census. *United States Census of Population: 1960.* Vol. I. *Characteristics of the Population,* pt. 35 *North Carolina.* Washington, D.C.: Government Printing Office, 1963.

_____. Office of Business Economics. *Survey of Current Business* 49 (April, 1969).

U.S. Department of Health, Education and Welfare. Public Health Service. *Vital Statistics of the United States, 1964,* vol. II, *Mortality.* Washington, D.C.: Government Printing Office, 1966.

U.S. Department of Labor. *Manpower Report of the President for 1967.* Washington, D.C.: Government Printing Office, 1967.

_____. *Manpower Report of the President for 1969.* Washington, D.C.: Government Printing Office, 1969.

_____. *1969 Statistics on Manpower: A Supplement to the Manpower Report of the President.* Washington, D.C.: Government Printing Office, 1969.

_____. *1966 Report of the Secretary of Labor on Manpower Research and Training under the Manpower Development and Training Act of 1962.* Washington, D.C.: Government Printing Office, 1966.

_____. Bureau of Employment Security. U.S. Employment Service. *Estimates of Worker Traits Requirements for 4000 Jobs.* Washington, D.C.: Government Printing Office, 1956.

_____. Office of the Manpower Administrator. *Manpower Administration Notice No. 3-66.* Washington, D.C.: U.S. Department of Labor, 1966.

U.S. Equal Employment Opportunity Commission. *Negro Employment in the Textile Industries of North and South Carolina,* by Donald D. Osburn. Washington, D.C.: Equal Employment Opportunity Commission, 1966.

U.S. President. *Economic Report of the President, 1964, together with the Annual Report of the Council of Economic Advisors.* Washington, D.C.: Government Printing Office, 1964.

_____. *Economic Report of the President, 1970, together with the Annual Report of the Council of Economic Advisors.* Washington, D.C.: Government Printing Office, 1970.

Weicher, John C. "The Effect of Income on Delinquency: Comment." *American Economic Review* 60 (March, 1970): 249-56.

Weisbrod, Burton A. "Concepts of Costs and Benefits." In *Problems in Public Expenditure Analysis,* edited by Samuel B. Chase, Jr., pp. 257-62. Washington, D.C.: The Brookings Institution, 1968.

_____. "Education and Investment in Human Capital." *Journal of Political Economy* 70 (Supplement, October, 1962): 106-23

Bibliography

————. *External Benefits of Public Education: An Economic Analysis.* Princeton, N.J.: Princeton University, Department of Economics, Industrial Relations Section, 1964.

————. "Income Redistribution Effects and Benefit-Cost Analysis." In *Problems in Public Expenditure Analysis,* edited by Samuel B. Chase, Jr., pp. 177-209. Washington, D.C.: The Brookings Institution, 1968.

Weiss, Leonard W. "Concentration and Labor Earnings." *American Economic Review* 56 (March, 1966): 96-117.

Welch, Finis. "Education in Production." *Journal of Political Economy* 78 (February, 1970): 35-59.

————. "Measurement of the Quality of Schooling." *American Economic Review* 56 (May, 1966): 379-92.

Yohe, William P., and Karnosky, Denis S. "Interest Rates and Price Level Changes, 1952-69." *Federal Reserve Bank of St. Louis Review* 51 (December, 1969): 18-38.